THE MIND
OF THE
MASTER

ABOUT THE AUTHOR

Robert E. Coleman is the McCreless Professor of Evangelism at Asbury Theological Seminary. The graduate curriculum which he has developed over 23 years of teaching is recognized internationally for its excellence. He has served as President of the Academy for Evangelism in Theological Education, and is presently the Chairman of the North American Lausanne Committee on World Evangelization. His Bible study and discipleship books are being used in sixty languages around the world.

Robert E. Coleman

THE MIND OF THE MASTER

Fleming H. Revell Company
Old Tappan, New Jersey

Second Printing

30,000 copies in print in English editions.
This book is also available in Chinese,
Hindi and Urdu translations.

Library of Congress Cataloging in Publication Data

Coleman, Robert Emerson, date
   The mind of the Master.

   Includes bibliographical references.
   1. Jesus Christ—Person and offices. I. Title.
BT202.C63   232   77-7351
ISBN 0-8007-0879-2
ISBN 0-8007-0880-6 pbk.

Contents

Introduction   7

1   His Source of Life   21

2   His Communion Through Prayer   37

3   His Word of Authority   53

4   His Understanding of the Gospel   69

5   His Way of the Cross   85

6   His Heavenly Vision   102

Epilogue   119

Take my yoke upon you, and learn of
me . . . .

Matthew 11:29

Introduction

Making Disciples

Jesus calls men to learn of Him. We are invited to discipleship, to enroll in His school of obedience.[1] While this life of faith has a beginning, it never ends. Every day confronts us with new discovery and challenge. And as we apply to our hearts what we learn, we have the joy of being progressively conformed to His image.

By placing the emphasis on becoming like Him, our Lord assures the believer not only growth into His character, but participation in His continuing ministry. No one can follow Jesus without becoming involved in what He is doing. Invariably, then, disciples become fishers of men (Matt. 4:19; Mark 1:17; Luke 5:10).

Increasingly this expectation was spelled out by Jesus as He worked with His first disciples (Matt. 10:1—11:1; Mark 3:14, 15; 6:7–13; Luke 6:13–16; 9:1–6; 10:1–24), culminating in the post-Resurrection commands (Matt. 28:19, 20; Mark 16:15; Luke 24:47, 48; Acts 1:8; John 20:21; cf. 17:18). The disciples

---

[1] The word *disciple* (μαθητής) describes a learner, as in the sense of an apprentice or student. Though the term can be applied in any master-pupil relationship, as used in the Gospels it usually denotes those persons who follow Christ, and "always implies the existence of a personal attachment which shapes the whole of life of the one described." *Theological Dictionary of the New Testament,* ed. Gerhard Kittel, trans. and ed. Geoffrey W. Bromiley, IV (Grand Rapids: Wm. B. Eerdmans Co., 1967), p. 441. See also Paul Sevier Minear, *The Images of the Church in the New Testament* (London: Littenworth, 1960), pp. 145–148.

were to go into the world as His representatives on a mission like His own: witnessing to the Gospel of salvation. And just as they had been discipled, so they were to disciple others, teaching them in turn to do the same, until through this process of multiplication, their witness reached the uttermost parts of the earth.[2]

This is His strategy to win the world, so unassuming in its simplicity, yet invincible in its ultimate triumph. The initial thrust is upon evangelism, since disciples cannot be made without hearing the good news of salvation.[3] But merely delivering the message is not enough. Persons must be nurtured who will continue to grow in Jesus, reproducing their lives along the way.[4] Making disciples is of necessity the mandate of the great commission.[5]

---

[2] This concept is developed in my study *The Master Plan of Evangelism* (Old Tappan, N.J.: Fleming H. Revell, 1963, 1964). The book notes a number of other sources which treat the subject, the most comprehensive being A. B. Bruce's classic *The Training of the Twelve* (New York: Richard R. Smith, 1930 © 1871). Also outstanding is Henry Latham, *Pastor Pastorium* (Cambridge: Deighton Ball and Co., 1910). A brief overview is in my A. W. Pippert Lecture at Nyack, "The Pattern of a Fruitful Life," in *Evangelism in Perspective* (Harrisburg: Christian Publications, 1976), pp. 49–70.

[3] The word *evangelize* in the New Testament means "to spread good news," though it takes on a larger reference when put into a theological context. A good definition appears in the Lausanne Covenant, which concludes that evangelism "is the proclamation of the historical, Biblical Christ as Saviour and Lord, with a view to persuading people to come to Him personally and so be reconciled to God." Article 4.

[4] Again the Lausanne Covenant states this principle so clearly: "In issuing the Gospel invitation we have no liberty to conceal the cost of discipleship. Jesus still calls all who would follow Him to deny themselves, take up their cross, and identify themselves with the new community. The results of evangelism include obedience to Christ, incorporation into his church and responsible service in the world" (Article 4). John Stott in his commentary on this article notes that "the objective of evangelism is conversion, and implies a radical change of life." *The Lausanne Covenant* (Minneapolis: World Wide Publication, 1975), p. 24. A further amplification of this definition is by Michael Cassidy, "The Nature of Evangelism," in *The New Evangelicalism, An International Symposium on the Lausanne Covenant*, ed. C. Rene Padilla (Downers Grove: InterVarsity, 1976), pp. 67–86. Whether this kind of commitment is a consequence of evangelism, or is inherent in it, makes little difference to me. What

Everyone Has a Part

Every believer is needed in this work. Whether one is considered clergy or lay makes no difference.[6] In the sight of our Lord, every disciple is a ministering servant. When this is forgotten the priesthood of all believers is confounded, if not paralyzed. To be sure, there are diversities of gifts and offices, but all members of the Body of Christ are called to minister through their own endowments and vocations.[7]

---

matters is that the Gospel proclamation not be seen as an activity in isolation from what follows. For a discussion of this point from different perspectives see both John Stott's *Christian Mission in the Modern World* (Downers Grove: InterVarsity Press, 1971), pp. 35–57; and Peter Wagner, *Frontiers in Missionary Strategy* (Chicago: Moody, 1971), pp. 15–47.

[5] The Matthean version (28:19, 20) especially brings this out, where the only verb in the passage, μαθητεύσατε, literally translates "make disciples." *Go, baptize,* and *teach* are all participles, which means that they derive their force from the leading verb, though the word *go* does stand in a coordinate relationship to the dominant verb. This command clarifies the parallel account in Mark 16:15, where "preach the Gospel" also appears in the same verb form. So whether going, preaching, baptizing, or teaching, the objective is the making of Christian disciples. Note the comment in *The Master Plan of Evangelism,* pp. 108, 109.

[6] One of the most refreshing winds of the Spirit in our time, paralleling renewed interest in the Scriptures, is a resurgence of the lay ministry in virtually every sector of Christendom. Some who have written in the field include Roland Allen, Elton Trueblood, Paul Rees, Stephen Neill, Samuel Shoemaker, David Haney, Tom Allan, Eugene Sterner, Richard C. Halverson, Gains S. Dobbins, Kenneth Chafin, W. Dayton Roberts, and Thomas Mullen. Limited bibliographies related to the theme will be found in Frederick K. Wentz, *The Laymen's Role* (New York: Doubleday and Co., 1963); and Mark Gibbs and T. Ralph Morton, *God's Lively People* (Philadelphia: The Westminster Press, 1971).

[7] Related to the renewed attention to the laity is the exercise of spiritual gifts within the Body. Interested persons may want to peruse the growing literature in this subject by such representative authors as Ray C. Stedman, J. Oswald Sanders, Kenneth Kinghorn, Agnes Sanford, Larry Christenson, Elizabeth O'Conner, William McRae, Rick Yohn, W. T. Purkiser, Donald Gee, Bill Gothard, Richard F. Houts, and Arnold Billinger, among others. In this connection, Peter Gillquist's statement on the gifts, *Let's Quit Fighting about the Holy Spirit* (Grand Rapids: Zondervan, 1974), tactfully points out where problems can arise, and offers some good counsel.

Nowhere is this truth more pertinent than in discharging Jesus' last commission, a task which is not dependent upon a particular ministering gift, though it utilizes them all. The evangelist, for example, may bring multitudes to decision, and thereby precipitate the growing process.[8] But the slow, painstaking task of disciple making is scarcely begun in evangelistic campaigns. The same could be said of the pulpit ministry in Sunday worship services. This is not to depreciate these special ministries, for they serve a vital function in the Body. Making disciples, however, comes largely through day-by-day personal relationships, which means that the gifted evangelist or pastor has no more discipling opportunity with those few persons closely associated with him than does the factory worker or housewife in their small sphere of fellowship. When this is grasped, the thrill of fulfilling the great commission comes within the reach of the daily experience of every child of God.

Equipping the Saints

That so few Christians share this excitement and sense of destiny reflects the superficial way we have been equipped for the ministry.[9] Most churchmen have simply no com-

---

[8] A distinction may be made between the evangelistic gift, allotted a few, and the general work of evangelism which belongs to the total Church. The specialized word *evangelist, εὐαγγελιστής,* occurs only three times in the New Testament (Acts 21:8; Eph. 4:11; 2 Tim. 4:5); while the broader terms *evangelize* or *preach the Gospel, εὐαγγελίζω,* and the noun form *evangel* or *gospel, εὐαγγελιον,* are used about 130 times. Normally the more common words are applied to Christ and the apostles, but they are also used in reference to the whole Christian community (e.g., Acts 5:42; 8:4), and with a strong emphasis upon obligation (Mark 13:10; 14:9; 16:15; Matt. 24:14; 26:13). It is fortunate that God gives some to the church who have a particular effectiveness communicating to those outside the fellowship, a ministry which may involve itinerating from place to place. These evangelists fill an essential place in the total ministry of the body. However, most Christians manifest other gifts, and though all share the same compulsion to bear witness to their faith and bring people to Christ, evangelism will find its most satisfying expression in that area of their proficiency.

[9] Much has been made of Ephesians 4:11, 12, which states that God "gave some to be apostles, some to be prophets, some to be

prehension of laboring together with Christ in reconciling the
world to God. One wonders how the Church could be so re-
miss in her teaching! Merely providing Sunday-school classes
and beautifully illustrated instruction manuals, however
commendable, can hardly be considered sufficient. Believers
need personal training in how to share their faith and disciple
others. Where adequate instruction is denied, potentially
fruitful ministers flounder in aimlessness, eventually despair-
ing of their usefulness.

The believing community might offer more assistance if its
institutional forms were not so inflexible and mechanical. Seldom does one find within the system that spontaneity, fellowship, and mutual sharing of gifts so necessary for dynamic
discipleship. In light of the biblical pattern, the Church could
well afford to rethink its structures, giving greater attention to
the home and the daily common life.[10]

Yet, the problem of inertia probably goes deeper, its roots
reaching into the individual's basic attitudes. Outside conditions, however disappointing, should not be able to stifle the
joyous calling to share the grace of God. The question is

---

evangelists, and some to be pastors and teachers, to prepare God's
people for works of service" (NIV). It is clear that these gifted leaders
have a primary function to equip believers for ministry. A good amplification of this passage, and its implications for the Church, is in
Roy J. Fish's updated work of J. E. Conant, *Every Member
Evangelism for Today* (New York: Harper & Row, 1976, © 1922), pp.
14–18. See also my note in *The Master Plan of Evangelism*, p. 34. A
recent presentation of the concept, especially helpful in discussing
some of the problems which may arise in the Church, is Paul Benja-
min's *The Equipping Ministry* (Cincinnati: Standard, 1977).

[10] Again, this is a subject which many have addressed in recent
years. Churchmen who have made contributions, in addition to those
mentioned in earlier notes, include Lawrence Richards, William
George Olsen, Robert S. Girard, Gene A. Getz, David R. Maines, C.
Watchman Nee, Ralph Neighbor, Stuart D. Briscoe, John Westerhoff,
Lyle Schaller, Findley Edge, Daniel Baumann, Donald J. MacNair,
Robert H. Schuller, and Hollis L. Green. For an excellent overall
presentation, with a helpful bibliography, see Howard A. Snyder,
The Problem of Wine Skins (Downers Grove: InterVarsity Press,
1975). Also helpful is the material on church growth, of which
Donald A. McGavran's *Understanding Church Growth* (Grand
Rapids: W. B. Eerdmans Co., 1970) is probably the best introduction
to the field.

finally one of motivation. Unless making disciples is a compulsion within the heart, it is unlikely that any external program will effect lasting results. That is why disciples must, above all else, grow in the knowledge of the Lord (Eph. 4:13), so to think thoughts after Him.

The Master Teacher

I have no hesitancy in affirming that all truth centers in Jesus Christ. He is the eternal Word by which God makes Himself and His purposes known, and the Son in whom the fulness of God's love forever dwells. In order to know anything of ultimate reality, we must learn of Him. Apart from Christ, there is nothing but futility, and we see only confusion in the course of history.

What makes Him the supreme focus of study is the fusion of His divine and human nature in one common self.[11] Such a life admits to examination under the closest scrutiny. While we cannot fathom the will of the Father, nor analyze the outreach of the Spirit, we can *see* Jesus (Heb. 2:9). He is a man—fully divine but nevertheless a man with all the essential ingredients of humanity.

In our likeness, yet as God, Jesus can say: "I am the way, and the truth, and the life; no one comes to the Father, but by me" (John 14:6 RSV).[12] As a paraphrase of this text, Grotius offers: "I am the example, the teacher, the giver of eternal

---

[11] It should be understood that the union of God was not with a human person, but with a human nature. This nature which Christ acquired received its personality by virtue of its union with Him. Within His own unique selfhood, the divine and human natures of Christ each retain their respective properties and functions, without either alternation of essence or interference with the other. As to how this was done, some suggest an intercommunication between the human and divine natures; others imagine a connecting link, such as gifts of the Holy Spirit. Whatever view one may hold, Christ possessed two natures, but only one personality. The varying modes of consciousness may pass quickly from the divine to the human, but the person is always the same.

[12] Jesus often affirmed His divine relationship with the Father, clearly establishing His own consciousness of deity. He claimed heavenly origin (John 8:23; 17:5); and oneness with God (John 5:17; 10:14, 15; 11:27; 14:9). He asserted His sinlessness (John 8:46). He proclaimed Himself Master of heavenly hosts (e.g., Matt. 13:41;

life." Luther read it: "I am the beginning, the middle, and the end of the ladder to heaven"; while Augustine subordinated the last attributes to the first to make it read simply: "I am the true way of life." However we may prefer to interpret the words, this much is clear—Jesus sets forth Himself as the object of our faith and the pattern of our life.[13]

This is the basis of His approach in discipling men. He does not ask us to follow a theory, but to follow a Person. His life is the illustration of what He wants His disciples to become.

The Measure of Behavior

Hence, the quest of our lives should be to know Him; to share His deepest feelings, His joys, His dreams; to know "the power of his resurrection, and the fellowship of his sufferings, being made comfortable unto his death" (Phil. 3:10). Such an obsession should not be considered strange; it is only natural for a disciple to want the mind of his teacher.

The truth is that only as we know Christ can we understand ourselves. This is why the behavioral sciences, which base their findings upon the study of fallen man, offer no sure directives for human conduct.[14] For the measure of our true selves

---

16:27), while making evil spirits subject to Him (e.g., Luke 11:20). His followers were asked to give to Him the sacrifice and devotion they would give to God (e.g., Matt. 10:18, 37, 39); and He accepted worship from them. The authority of heaven and earth was claimed as His (Matt. 28:18); and in the exercise of this power He forgave sins, offered eternal life and peace, raised the dead, and promised to send the Holy Spirit. If Jesus did not hesitate to declare His experience with the Father, we should not be reluctant to testify of our relationship to Him.

[13] Quoted in John Peter Lange, *Commentary on the Holy Scriptures, John,* trans. Philip Schaff (Grand Rapids: Zondervan, n.d.), p. 437.

[14] I have no intention of belittling the data accumulated by these disciplines, but I merely point out that for the most part they have ignored Christian revelation in projecting their hypotheses. Recognizing their humanistic orientation, however, the discriminating student can learn much from such research. Of particular interest to the concern of this book is the study of motivational theory and values development. Just let it be understood that all naturalistic systems of thought, notwithstanding their insights, must finally come under the judgment of God's disclosure of truth in His own immutable Word.

we must look to Christ, the perfect Man, in whom we live and move and have our being. Wisely did Pascal envision his Lord saying:

> Compare not thyself with others, but with Me. If thou dost not find Me in those with whom thou comparest thyself, thou comparest thyself to one who is abominable. If thou findest Me in them, compare thyself to Me. But whom wilt thou compare? Thyself, or Me in thee? If it is thyself, it is one who is abominable. If it is I, thou comparest Me to thyself. Now I am God in all.[15]

To say that Jesus is the perfect prototype of our lives does not imply that we are saved by following His example. It only establishes the goal to which all our energies should be devoted. There was a uniqueness about His existence on earth, of course, which must be recognized in making contemporary application. However, in principle, we have in His teaching and manner of living all the necessary guidelines for our conduct.[16] When Jesus is clearly the model which in dependence upon grace we endeavor to pattern our lives, we will always grow in holiness, even if our human teachers and surrounding peer group fail to give any encouragement. In this sense, we can understand Thomas à Kempis speaking of "the imitation of Christ." [17]

---

[15] Blaise Pascal, *Pensées* (New York: E. P. Dutton and Co., 1958, p. 151). This collection of more than nine hundred thoughts by the devout French scientist, written about 1660, is one of literature's most profound insights to human experience from the perspective of Christian commitment. No student should miss reading it.

[16] Exact comparisons require identical conditions. For this reason, there are some specific practices of Christ which may not be applicable in our circumstances, like His example of celibacy. It should be honestly admitted, too, that in countless instances we do not know what He did, or would do, if He were in our place today. Charles Sheldon's question, "What would Jesus do?" cannot always be answered in a definitive way. Take the case of voting in a national election, or arbitrating a labor dispute. The example He gives rather establishes basic principles of behavior upon which we often must make the specific application.

[17] The classic by this name, first published in 1418, has probably exerted a larger influence upon the Church than any other devotional

Object of the Book

This book seeks to focus on some aspects of Christ's interior life. As such, it is essentially a study in His thoughts, not the method of His ministry. Although the two go together in practice, in theory, at least, being precedes doing.

Genuine witness is but the reflection of Christian experience. It can neither be worked up through emotional appeals nor engineered through clever organization. Hence, to the degree that we share the mind of Christ, and feel His passion for the Kingdom—to that degree His ministry comes alive. When it does, the product is not forced into some stereotyped form or divorced from everyday occupation, but is clothed in the authentic shape of each unique personality and in the setting of one's own life-style.

To comprehend what this means, the present study proposes to look closely at the Saviour, trying to discern in Him those inner resources which gave direction and strength to His redeeming work among us. What were the wellsprings out of which His evangelism flowed? Why did He give Himself for an uncaring world? How could He keep going when all the armies of hell were massed against Him? If we can locate the sources of His power, we shall also discover our own.

References for Study

Strangely, little has been written on the mind of Christ from the standpoint of the great commission. The general treatments of Christ's life and teaching may bear upon His motivational thought, but seldom is the subject developed within the context of our special interest.[18] On the other hand, those

---

writing. A good modern version, based upon the English translation of Richard Whitford around 1530, is edited with an introduction by Harold C. Gardiner (New York: Image Books, 1955). Though the book has a limited doctrinal foundation, and was written originally for monks, it exposes a depth of humility and love which all of us need to hear again and again.

[18] A brief introduction to the general study of the life of Christ from an evangelical perspective is Donald Guthrie, *A Shorter Life of Christ* (Grand Rapids: Zondervan, 1970). Appended to the book is a good annotated bibliography of major works in the field. For com-

works which deal particularly with evangelizing the world
usually concentrate upon techniques and strategies with little
attention to the underlying mind-set of Christ. We can be
grateful for the valuable insight afforded in these works, many
of which are noted in the course of these pages, but still there
is room for an approach with the scope and purpose of this
book.

While trying to be abreast of what others have written, my
primary study has centered upon the inspired Scriptures, particularly the Gospel narratives.[19] An effort has been made
throughout to let Jesus speak for Himself, seeking as far as
possible to hear His words in the setting in which they were
uttered.[20] I cannot claim that the effort has always succeeded,
but it has been sincere.

---

parison, a presentation of the same subject from a liberal perspective
is Hans Conzelmoun, *Jesus* (Philadelphia: Fortress Press, 1973),
which also contains an annotated bibliography compiled by John
Reumann. One should not overlook, either, works in specialized
areas of Jesus' life, like prayer or evangelistic methodology, which at
their point of concentration are intensely helpful to our study. There
are also any number of books of a devotional nature which develop
themes around Christ. One of these, *Like Christ* by Andrew Murray
(New York: Grosset and Dunlap, n.d.), has been of inestimable blessing to me.

[19] With due respect to those who differ, I accept the Gospels as
written as an inerrant portrayal of the life of Christ. While not unmindful of historical problems pointed out by modern critics, it is not
within the scope of this study to argue for the validity of the Text. If
one would like to acquaint himself with the areas of controversy, the
issues are considered by recognized evangelical scholars in Donald
Guthrie, *New Testament Introduction,* 2nd Ed. (London: Tyndale
Press, 1970); F. F. Bruce, *The New Testament Documents: Are They
Reliable?* 5th Ed. (London: InterVarsity Press, 1960); and by the
same author, *New Testament History* (London: Nelson, 1969). On the
popular level, J. B. Phillips, *Ring of Truth* (London: Hodder, 1967),
is very helpful.

[20] My old Princeton New Testament professor, Dr. Otto Piper,
called this "biblical realism." It is the attempt to understand the
Bible from the perspective of the authors in the mind-set of their day.
Only after this is done can the application be cast in the contemporary application. If the miraculous nature of His life does not corre-
spond with our experience, it is not because this quality was added
by the community of believers, but because it was present in Jesus.

Selected Principles

Let it be admitted, too, that the attempt of a finite mind to encompass a theme so vast has in it an element of presumption. No book, or library of books, can ever exhaust the study of the infinite resources of our Lord. At best, only a few aspects of His life can be touched upon, though it is hoped these sketches will give some feel for the whole.

I have concentrated upon six areas of the Master's thought, each pointing to a basic truth in which He disciples us. All the concepts are interrelated, but they are considered separately in order to provide structure and sequence to the study.

In making applications to our experience, I am aware of the human tendency to stress one facet of character to the neglect of another. A perceptive teacher has noted:

> Men undertake to be spiritual, and then become ascetic; or, endeavoring to hold a liberal view of comforts and pleasures of society, they are soon buried in the world, and slaves to its fashions; or, holding a scrupulous watch to keep out every particular sin, they become legal, and fall out of liberty; or, charmed with the noble and heavenly liberty, they run to negligence and irresponsible living; so the earnest become violent, the fervent fanatical and censorious, the gentle waver, the firm turn bigots, the liberal grow lax, the benevolent ostentatious.[21]

Perfect balance, I suppose, is never attained in our twisted estate. Yet while we must continue to make adjustments, it is comforting to know that our Teacher needs no improvements,

---

[21] Horace Bushnell, *Nature and Supernatural as Together Constituting the One System of God* (New York: Charles Scribner's Sons, 1886), p. 288. Some developments of Bushnell's theology and educational theory can be questioned by orthodox theologians, but his beautiful insights to the life of Christ can still be enchanting, as is especially true of the chapter out of which this quotation is taken, "The Character of Jesus Forbids His Possible Classification with Men," pp. 276–332.

no extravagance corrected. "The balance of His character is never disturbed, or readjusted, and the astounding assumption on which it is based is never shaken, even by a suspicion that He falters in it." [22]

A Humbling Effort

Needless to say, the discipline involved in preparing this book has been a searching experience. No one can look very long upon Immanuel's face and remain the same. Far from supporting any sense of accomplishment in my calling, gazing upon His glory has shown me how far short of the ideal I remain. Times beyond number I have had to turn from my desk and fall on my knees in confession and renewed dedication.

So, in a personal way, this has been for me a spiritual exercise. It has made me face myself in Christ, and seek to align my life with His. I offer it to you, not as a record of my accomplishment, but as a guide to my aspirations.

If you would like to know what the goal is worth, may I suggest that you read the last chapter first. After all, this follows the biblical precedent, where the end is known from the beginning.

---

[22] *Ibid.*

It is the spirit that gives life, the flesh is of no avail . . . .

John 6:63 RSV

1
His Source of Life

The Evangel became flesh and blood through the Holy Spirit. By the same power, God transforms our lives and molds them in the image of His Son. However viewed, the impartation of the divine nature is clearly the Spirit's work. Here, then, is a good place to begin our study.

The Miraculous Conception

In the fulness of time, God's plan to take upon Himself the experience of man assumed material form in the incarnation of Christ. He "sent forth his Son, made of a woman . . ." (Gal. 4:4). The new Being was not a man who became God; He is God who became man, coming into history from the outside. "So the word of God became a human being and lived among us" (John 1:14 PHILLIPS).

How could this happen? That was the question posed by the virgin Mary when told that she would be with child (Luke 1:29–34). The angel's answer was very clear: "The Holy Spirit will come upon you, and the power of the Most High will overshadow you; therefore the child to be born will be called holy, the Son of God" (Luke 1:35 RSV; cf. Exod. 13:12). So the handmaiden of the Lord "was found to be with child of the Holy Spirit" (Matt. 1:18 RSV). Mary's betrothed husband, the righteous Joseph, was given the same assurance: ". . . that which is conceived in her is of the Holy Spirit" (Matt. 1:20 RSV).[1]

---

[1] Due to the private and personal nature of this event, understandably the testimony of Scripture had to be very explicit. Jesus of Nazareth had no father in the flesh, though it is not suggested that this fact was commonly understood by the people at large (for exam-

The awesome sense of the Spirit's presence overflowed upon others close to the holy family. Upon hearing Mary's salutation, her cousin Elisabeth was filled with the Holy Spirit, blessing the Christ child's mother and the fruit of her womb (Luke 1:41–45). Likewise, Elisabeth's husband Zacharias was filled with the Spirit and prophesied of the Redeemer (Luke 1:67–80). Later the aged Simeon, also directed by the Spirit, took the child in his arms and praised God that his eyes had seen his salvation (Luke 2:25–32). Clearly the Scriptures emphasize that the Holy Spirit overshadowed Christ's birth.

Enabling Power

In view of God's work in the world from the very beginning, this should come as no surprise. The Third Member of the Holy Trinity has always been present, accomplishing His creative and redemptive purpose. What God plans as the Father, and reveals as the Son, He effects through the Spirit.[2]

---

ple, Matt. 13:55; Luke 2:27, 41, 43). The development of His physical body was like that of any other child born of a woman. But the inception of His life, with the formation of His perfect humanity, was the direct imposition of God's Spirit. However modern skeptics may seek to discount the witness of the Gospel writers, there is no other explanation for the Incarnation given in Scripture. An able discussion of the issues involved in this doctrine may be found in J. Gresham Machen, *The Virgin Birth of Christ* (New York: Harper & Row, 1930). Other good treatments are by James Orr, *The Virgin Birth of Christ* (New York: Charles Scribner's, 1907); Howard A. Hanke, *The Validity of the Virgin Birth* (Grand Rapids: Zondervan, 1963); and Robert G. Gromacke, *The Virgin Birth: Doctrine of Deity* (New York: Nelson, 1974). Perhaps the most unique approach to the matter is the beloved Frank C. Laubach's last published work, *Did Mary Tell Jesus Her Secret?* (London: Marshall, Morgan and Scott, 1970).

[2] Any formulation of the triune nature of God proves inadequate, for the very reason that human intelligence cannot explain the divine mind. Yet only by the Trinity can the Person and Mind of God be understood. As an attempt to define the reality, John Bunyan's witness shows a keen sensitivity: "From eternity, God was sole existing, but not solitary . . . . The Godhead is neither confused in unity, nor divided in number; there is a priority of order, but no superiority among the sacred persons . . . . They are equally possessed of the same divine excellence, and the same divine empire, and are equally the object of the same divine adoration." *The World to Come,* or

Within the Godhead, the Spirit completes the Personality of the Father and the Son; outside of God, in the world and in man, He communicates the divine will.[3]

We are introduced to Him in the very creation of the cosmos, when it is said "the Spirit of God moved upon the face of the waters" (Gen. 1:2; cf. Ps. 104:30). God then fashioned man in His image, and breathed into him this principle of life (Gen. 2:7; Job 33:4).[4] Not only in the beginning, but in the preserva-

---

Visions of Heaven and Hell, included in *Grace Abounding to the Chief of Sinners* (Philadelphia: W. A. Leary, n.d.), p. 240.

[3] For a thorough development of this doctrine, consult a good systematic or biblical theology. There are also scores of specialized treatments appealing to many different interests. Among the more general works are Abraham Kuyper, *The Work of the Holy Spirit* (New York: Funk and Wagnalls, 1900); Arthur Cleveland Downer, *The Mission and Ministration of the Holy Spirit* (Edinburgh: T. and T. Clark, 1909); W. T. Dawson, *The Indwelling Spirit* (London: Hodder and Stoughton, 1911); A. J. Gordon, *The Ministry of the Spirit* (Philadelphia: Judson, 1949, © 1894); Joseph Parker, *The Paraclete* (New York: Scribner, Armstrong and Co., 1875); Arthur Pink, *The Holy Spirit* (Grand Rapids: Baker, 1970); and David M. Howard's compact *By the Power of the Holy Spirit* (Downers Grove: InterVarsity, 1973). Some take more of a theological approach, like Charles Carter, *The Person and Ministry of the Holy Spirit* (Grand Rapids: Baker, 1974), reflecting a Wesleyan perspective; while a companion volume of the same name and publisher by Edwin H. Palmer represents the traditional Calvinistic viewpoint. Also from the Reformed stance is Frederick Dale Bruner, *A Theology of the Holy Spirit* (Grand Rapids: W. B. Eerdmans, 1970), a critique of the Pentecostal position. Other books are more devotional in character, like Andrew Murray, *The Spirit of Christ* (London: Nesbet and Co., Ltd., 1880); or Octavius Winslow, *The Work of the Holy Spirit* (London: The Banner of Truth Trust, 1972 © 1840). These, and many other sources, assure no lack of material for the discerning student who wants to pursue the subject. Extensive bibliographies may be found in Charles Carter, op. cit., pp. 337–350, and F. D. Bruner, op. cit., pp. 365–376.

[4] Interestingly, the word *breath* in the Hebrew is the root for the word *Spirit.* Literally, then, in breathing upon him, God spiritualized man. That is why he became a living soul. Altogether there are about a hundred references to the Spirit in the Old Testament. A concise tracing of these accounts may be found in James Elder Cumming, *Through the Eternal Spirit* (Chicago: Fleming H. Revell, 1896). More developed is Leon J. Wood, *The Holy Spirit in the Old Testament* (Grand Rapids: Zondervan, 1976).

tion and sustenance of His creatures, the Spirit is the link between God and the created order (Ps. 143:10; Isa. 59:21; 63:11; Ezek. 36:27; 37:13, 14; 39:29; Neh. 9:20; Hag. 2:5). And when divine fellowship is broken through man's disobedience, the Spirit strives with the rebellious soul, seeking reconciliation with the creature of His love (Gen. 6:3; Ps. 51:11; 139:7; Isa. 30:1; 63:10; Acts 7:51). Making a holy people is always His concern.

Some individuals are specially prepared by the Spirit to perform needed ministries. Joseph was such a person during his sojourn in Egypt (Gen. 41:38). Likewise, the Spirit inspired Moses' leadership in the wilderness, as well as the seventy men who assisted Moses in bearing the people's burdens (Num. 11:17, 24, 25, 29). Through the same Spirit, others were qualified to serve as craftsmen in building and furnishing the tabernacle (Exod. 28:3; 31:3–5; 35:31–35). Later judges and kings were equipped for their roles in the same manner (Num. 27:18; Judg. 3:10; 6:34; 11:29; 14:6, 19; 15:14; 1 Sam. 10:6; 11:6; 16:13). These people were not always faithful to their trust, but insofar as they fulfilled God's calling, it was the Spirit who gave them strength and wisdom.

The prophet illustrates this activity of the Spirit most completely. In the flesh, he was as other men, but on certain occasions the Spirit would come upon him and so activate his perception and quicken his ability to communicate that he could proclaim accurately the message of the Lord (Ezek. 11:5; 3:12, 14; 8:3; 11:1, 24; 43:5; Mic. 3:8; 2 Sam. 23:1, 2; cf. Matt. 22:43; Mark 12:36; Acts 1:16; 28:25). Our whole doctrine of biblical inspiration ultimately rests upon the fact that these men of God spoke as they were borne along by the Holy Spirit (2 Pet. 1:21; cf. 2 Tim. 3:16).

The key point is the power of God's personal enablement. His work cannot be done in the energy of the flesh. Only as human resources are under His control can His work be done. It is "not by might, nor by power, but by my spirit, saith the Lord of hosts" (Zech. 4:6).

The focus of this unfolding drama of redemption was the promised Messiah. He who was foreshadowed in the priestly offerings, typified in mighty acts of deliverance, and proclaimed in prophetic word, would someday dwell with His people in person. A virgin would conceive, and bear a son,

who would be called Immanuel—"God with us" (Isa. 7:14;
Matt. 1:23). Upon this Branch growing out of the root of David,
the Spirit of the Lord would rest without measure (Isa. 11:1,
2), and through Him a Messianic age was to dawn when the
Spirit finally would be poured forth upon all flesh (Isa. 32:18;
cf. Joel 2:28–32).

The Climactic Mission

That Christ should come through the Spirit's agency is thus
quite predictable. Though His incarnation was radically different in nature from anything that had happened before, it
preserved the continuity of God's age-long redemptive process. The Spirit who had been working faithfully for millen-
niums through chosen vessels, at special times, in limited degrees, now brought forth the Man of God in absolute and permanent fullness.

What was so prominent in Christ's birth received new stress
as He began His public ministry thirty years later. Anticipat-
ing His work, while distinguishing it from his own, John the
Baptist announced that Jesus would baptize with the Holy
Spirit and with fire (Matt. 3:11; Mark 1:8; Luke 3:16). These
words, pregnant with visions of the divine presence and
power, indicated the kind of ministry Christ would have. As
John later observed, "For the one whom God has sent speaks
the words of God; to him God gives the Spirit without limit"
(John 3:34 NIV).

When Jesus appeared at the river Jordan to be baptized by
John, the prophet hesitated to oblige, knowing that he was
unworthy to even loose Christ's shoes. But Jesus insisted, explaining that submission to this act was necessary to fulfill all
righteousness.[5] Then, having demonstrated obedience to the

---

[5] Why Jesus would request baptism of John has caused considerable speculation, particularly since the practice was described as a
baptism of repentance. Certainly the Lord had no sin to remit, as
would be true of others. For Jesus, then, it must have been an act of
identification of Himself with the people. His observance of this
ceremony was part of the process by which He was made sin for us (2
Cor. 5:21). Also, there may be significance in the way it associated
Jesus with the priestly function of His Messianic work, since it was
customary for Jewish priests to be inducted into office by baptism
(Exod. 29:4; cf. Heb. 5:6).

Father's will, the Holy Spirit descended upon Him, and a voice spoke from heaven, saying: "This is my beloved Son, in whom I am well pleased" (Matt. 3:13–17; Mark 1:9–11; Luke 3:21–23; cf. John 1:32–34). The seal of divine approval abode upon Him—publicly He was attested to be the divine Messenger, but more significantly, inwardly there was the full consciousness of that living bond of union He sustained with the Father.

Thereafter Jesus, "being full of the Spirit," left the scene of John's revival, "and was led by the Spirit into the wilderness" (Luke 4:1; Mark 1:12) "to be tempted of the devil" (Matt. 4:1). The Spirit's direction in this supernatural confrontation may be appreciated when the principle at issue emerges. The devil, in three exemplary ways, asked Christ to compromise the spiritual character of His mission by conforming to the popular expectations of the world. If He would only turn stones into bread to satisfy the physical appetite, a legitimate need, the multitudes would flock after Him. Or if He would openly leap from the pinnacle of the Temple so that God could miraculously save Him, such a spectacular sign would surely impress the people with His claims. In fact, if He would only arrange to work without upsetting the present world's system, He could have the glory of all the kingdoms of the earth. The appeal in each case is to take the easy course of self-indulgence in contrast to the hard, tedious, sacrificial way of self-denial. But Jesus was not to be deceived. He would not demean the Kingdom of God by adopting the methods of the flesh to attain it.[6] Supported by Scripture, He commanded Satan to depart (Matt. 4:2–11; Luke 4:2–13). Though the testings would be repeated later in other forms, the spiritual nature of His ministry was firmly established.

---

[6] These temptations, while not exhaustive, typify the avenue through which testings may come to all men (cf. Heb. 4:15). Of course, Jesus' circumstance was unique, since He alone had perfect knowledge and unlimited power. Nevertheless, granted that our capacity to experience such temptations is limited, we can recognize the same pressures in the world. It is well to observe, too, that the greatest temptations appeal to human strength, not human weakness. The subtle implications of Jesus' temptation will come out again in discussing His mission in chapter 5.

Ministering in the Spirit

Ready now to launch out in His public ministry, the Lord "returned in the power of the Spirit into Galilee" (Luke 4:14). So mighty was His work that soon His fame spread across the country, and He was "glorified of all" (Luke 4:15; cf. Matt. 4:17; Mark 1:14, 15).

Lest someone miss the source of His work, upon the first invitation to speak in His home synagogue at Nazareth, Jesus stood up and read from the scroll of Isaiah: "The Spirit of the Lord is on me; therefore he has anointed me to preach good news to the poor. He has sent me to proclaim freedom for the prisoners and recovery of sight for the blind, to release the oppressed, to proclaim the year of the Lord's favor" (Luke 4:18, 19, NIV; cf. Isa. 61:1–2). Having finished reading the passage, Jesus rolled up the parchment, gave it back to the attendant, then sat down and announced to the startled congregation, "Today this scripture is fulfilled in your hearing" (Luke 4:21 NIV).

He wanted everyone to know that what He did and said was not in the strength of man; it was in the power of the Holy Spirit.[7] Nothing about His ministry could be explained in naturalistic terms. This was quite shocking to most Jews of His day, for they commonly believed that the Spirit's activity in the world had ceased, and would not return until the end of the age.[8] Thus by associating His work with the Spirit, Jesus was saying that God was moving again among His people. It was an end to an era of alienation and the beginning of a time of grace. By the same criteria, He was also speaking God's final word to the world.

---

[7] In addition to the works already cited, one may find excellent treatment of Jesus' teaching about the Spirit's work in Louis Burton Crane, *The Teaching of Jesus Concerning the Holy Spirit* (New York: American Tract Society, 1905); J. Ritchie Smith, *The Holy Spirit in the Gospels* (New York: Macmillan, 1926); and Henry Barclay Swete, *The Holy Spirit in the New Testament* (Grand Rapids: Baker, 1976). A more critical approach, interesting by way of comparison, is J. E. Yates, *The Spirit and the Kingdom* (London: S.P.C.K., 1963).

[8] For a discussion of this point, see Joachim Jeremias, *New Testament Theology* (New York: Charles Scribner's Sons, 1971), pp. 80–85.

Those who rejected Christ, of course, were unwilling to accept His claims regarding the Spirit. To do so would require a recognition of His Messianic mission. So they had to account for His supernatural power some other way. On one occasion, following His healing of a demoniac, Jesus was accused by the Pharisees of being in league with the devil. Pointing out how ludicrous their reasoning was, He answered: "And if I drive out demons by Beelzebub, by whom do your people drive them out? So then, they will be your judges. But if I drive out demons by the Spirit of God, then the kingdom of God has come upon you" (Matt. 12:27, 28 NIV; cf. Luke 4:19, 20). Jesus was simply underscoring again the true source of His ministry. By closing their hearts to this fact, the unbelieving Jews were in danger of committing an unpardonable sin—they were blaspheming the Holy Spirit (Matt. 12:31, 32; Mark 3:28, 29; cf. Luke 11:14–26).[9]

The point is that the Spirit was ever present in the Son to make His life a revelation of God, both in deed and in word. Thus inwardly equipped, Jesus went about doing good, healing and teaching and preaching. Finally, as the sin offering for the world, "through the eternal Spirit [He] offered himself without blemish to God" as a sacrifice at Calvary (Heb. 9:14 RSV). His atoning work then finished, by the same mighty power, He was raised from the dead (Rom. 8:11), "and declared to be the Son of God" (Rom. 1:4).

Glorifying Jesus

The relationship between Christ and the Spirit is most beautifully exhibited in those last hours spent with His disciples before the Crucifixion (John 14:1—16:33). As they reclined around the table in the upper room after the Passover

---

[9] The term *blasphemy* (βλασφημία) comes from a word meaning to slander or to revile the reputation of someone. It is well to note that in this reference Jesus does not say that the Pharisees were beyond redemption, but by their hostile attitude they displayed a condition which, unless reversed, would bring final separation from God's mercy. To scorn Christ is to reject the only way of salvation, and hence, to be in a state of unforgiveness. If one persists in this rejection, the state of judgment becomes permanent—one is guilty of an eternal sin.

supper, Jesus reminded them that He would soon return to the
Father. But He assured His anxious followers that they need
not be troubled, for when He returned to heaven, the Spirit
would continue His work on earth.

Actually it was for their own good that Jesus went away.
While He was with them in bodily form, they saw little need
to rely upon the Spirit, and hence they had not come to know
intimately the deeper reality of His Life. In His absence,
however, they had no visible support. To survive they had to
learn the secret of His inner communion with the Father. Yet,
out of their necessity, they would experience greater fellowship with Christ than they had ever known before. For the
Spirit was not limited by time or space, as was Jesus in His
body, and hence they could always abide in His Presence.

Jesus called Him "another Comforter," indicating that the
Spirit would have a ministry with the disciples much like His
own (John 14:16).[10] He was not comparing Himself with a
theory or theological abstraction, but with a Person—One who
in the unseen realm would be as real among them as was Jesus
when they walked the trails of Galilee together. He would
guide them into truth (John 14:26; 16:14); He would answer
their questions (John 16:13, 25); He would show them things
to come (John 16:13). In short, He would take Christ's place
among them and continue His work (John 14:12; 16:14, 15;
15:26).

The ultimate purpose of all the Spirit's work is to glorify the
Son (John 15:26; 16:14). The Spirit never points to Himself.
Christ is the visible Word, the speaking Self, the Person in
whom the Father may be known. But we see Christ only
through the ministry of the Holy Spirit (1 John 4:2).

As the Spirit lifts up the Holy One, the world becomes
aware of its perverse nature (John 16:8–11). Men are convicted
of their sins of unbelief. They recognize in Christ's completed
work the only way we can appear righteous before a holy God.

---

[10] The word *Comforter* ($\pi\alpha\rho\acute{\alpha}\kappa\lambda\eta\tau\sigma\varsigma$) has the meaning of "one who
strengthens or stands beside," whereas the word *another* stresses the
sameness of quality between Christ's life and that of the Spirit. An
enlargement of this idea will be found in *The Master Plan of
Evangelism,* pp. 67–69; and G. Campbell Morgan, *The Teaching of
Christ* (New York; Revell, 1913), p. 65.

Moreover, the world's standard of truth is shown to be utterly in error. Jesus, condemned by the world, is seen exalted in heaven; whereas the prince of this earth, the devil, is cast down. How reassuring this is to evangelism! We can know that in spite of the world's blindness and indifference, Christ's work will not be defeated. The Spirit of God will bear witness to the truth, and draw men to the Saviour.

New Life in Christ

Responding to the Spirit's appeal, however, requires a whole new set of values. There must be a conversion; a change of direction; a turning from darkness into light (Matt. 18:3; John 5:24; cf. 1 Pet. 2:9). It is likened by Jesus to being "born again" (John 3:3). Left to our own resources, we have no way to experience true life. "Unless a man is born of water and the Spirit," Jesus said, "he cannot enter the kingdom of God. Flesh gives birth to flesh, but the Spirit gives birth to spirit. You should not be surprised at my saying, 'You must be born again'" (John 3:5–7 NIV).

The reference is to a divine regeneration, the impartation of a new life principle within the heart. Jesus is not speaking of a human reformation, though man cooperates with the birth process, and through the allusion to water, symbolic of washing away the past, underscores the condition of repentance (Luke 13:3). But the actual re-creation of personality belongs to God's initiative. "The Spirit gives life; the flesh counts for nothing" (John 6:63 NIV; cf. 1:13; Rom. 8:9, 12, 13; 2 Cor. 3:6, 7, 16; 5:17; Gal. 3:3; 5:12; 6:15; Col. 2:13; 1 Pet. 1:23; 2 Pet. 1:4; Heb. 12:10).

Thus what has been the inner source of life for Jesus becomes the means by which man may also experience communion with God. The same One who clothed the Word with perfect manhood infuses a fallen humanity with the divine nature. Man is still finite in all his resources, and bears the marks of a corrupted body, but he is no longer his own, and he begins to grow, however falteringly, in the likeness of another Person.

Growing in Christ

Having given birth to life, the indwelling Spirit continues to sustain and nourish His new creation. Jesus compares Him to a perpetual "well of water springing up into everlasting life" (John 4:14). The trusting heart can drink so fully from this fountain that "streams of living water will flow from within him" (John 7:38 NIV; cf. 7:39), overflowing in blessing to a watching world. By the same vitalizing power, latent natural talents and spiritual gifts come forth, enhancing both individuality and the common good.[11]

What is even better, communication with heaven restored, the spiritual person can authentically worship God, "in spirit and in truth" (John 4:23, 24; cf. Phil. 3:3). In this adoration, the human body becomes a "temple" of the *Holy* Spirit. This title, used by Jesus more than any other, accents His nature of holiness (Matt. 12:31; 28:19; Mark 3:29; 12:36; 13:11; Luke 11:13; 12:10, 12; John 14:26; 20:22; Acts 1:5, 8). It means that God is utterly separate from defilement. Nothing about His work can be associated with evil. Another name for the Spirit, "the Spirit of truth," emphasizes the absolute integrity of His Being; a fidelity which cannot be falsified (John 14:17; 15:26; 16:13; cf. 1 John 4:6).

With these qualities resident in the reborn man, we can see why life takes on a different character. Christlikeness shines through it all. The fruits of the Spirit invariably savor the disposition of Jesus (John 15:1–17; cf. Gal. 5:22, 23; Rom. 15:30; Col. 1:8), so that the Christian is progressively conformed to the image of his Lord (2 Cor. 3:18; 1 Pet. 1:2; 2 Thess. 2:13). Not that growth is always steady, for saints in the making encounter many trials, and may sometimes stagger in unbelief. The old fleshly nature does not easily capitulate. If not

---

[11] *Charismata* (χαρισματα), meaning "gifts of grace," in all their variety, belong to the ministry of the Spirit. The nature and use of spiritual gifts is not developed in the teachings of Jesus, though the subject is treated at length in the New Testament Epistles (e.g., 1 Cor. 12:1—14:40; Rom. 12:2–21; Eph. 4:7–16; and 1 Pet. 4:10, 11). The interested student might want to consult some of the popular readings in this field. However it would be well to remember Thomas à Kempis' observation that a wise lover "beholds not only the gifts but the Giver above all gifts." Op. cit., p. 110.

brought to the cross, it can rise up to cause all manner of trouble. Still, through it all, the precious Holy Spirit persists in His quest to mature a people in the knowledge of the Son of God, "attaining the full measure of perfection found in Christ" (Eph. 4:13 NIV).[12]

The fulness of the Spirit's work in man could not be appreciated until after Christ's work had been consummated on earth, and He had returned to heaven in His victorious state. Prior to this time, in the full dimension of His Life, the Spirit "was not yet given; because . . . Jesus was not yet glorified" (John 7:39).[13] But when Christ returned with our perfected nature into the holiest of all, "being by the right hand of God exalted," in full fellowship with that Life in which the Trinity dwells, He received from the Father the right to send the Holy Spirit upon His disciples in a measure which hitherto was not possible (Acts 2:33). It is in this fulness, as the very Presence of the crucified, resurrected and glorified God-man, that the Spirit of Jesus comes.

The Promised Power

We can understand why Jesus insisted that His disciples tarry until the promise became an experience (Luke 24:49; Acts 1:5, 8). He who had been Christ's strength all these years had to become real within them.[14] Unless they were pos-

---

[12] The phrase *in Christ* occurs about 150 times in the New Testament, principally in the writings of Paul. Among the many excellent treatments of the concept are John Ross MacDuff, *In Christo: The Monogram of St. Paul* (London: J. Nisbet, 1881); Arthur T. Pierson, *In Christ Jesus* (Chicago: Moody Press, 1974); and James S. Stewart, *A Man in Christ* (New York: Harper and Brothers, 1935).

[13] After the Resurrection, and before the Ascension, there is record that Jesus breathed on His disciples, and said, "Receive the Holy Spirit" (John 20:22 NIV). The reference seems to anticipate the outpouring of the Spirit at Pentecost, and is a sanction of the event. In this passage, Jesus also speaks of the disciples forgiving sin in others (John 20:23), an authority which He exercised, but which in the hands of the disciples can only be understood in conjunction with the Spirit's direction.

[14] Andrew Murray comments: "When the Holy Spirit came down, He brought as a personal Life within them what had previously only been a Life near them, but yet outside their own. The very Spirit of God's own Son, as He had lived and loved, had obeyed and died, was now to become their personal life." *The Spirit of Christ*, p. 149.

sessed by His living Presence, their lives would be forlorn of joy and peace, and the ministry of their Lord would never thrill their souls. Nothing less than an enduement of "power from on High," a baptism of consuming fire, would suffice for the task to which they were appointed.

Pentecost was the manifestation of the exalted Christ, and as such, the consummation of the Spirit's work through the ages. All that had gone before in the creation of man, in the making of Israel, and in the incarnate Life of Jesus was preparatory to this heavenly outpouring. In the heart of Spirit-filled man, the mission of Christ receives its fulfillment. Yet it was also the beginning of an era that will continue until Spirit-imbued witnesses bear the Gospel to the ends of the earth, and the King returns in glory. The Acts of the Apostles records how those early disciples, of one mind and heart, went on their way rejoicing, everywhere declaring what God had done.

Little wonder that the world was dismayed. Such undiluted joy, such spontaneous praise, such transparent love was awesome to behold. When beaten and stoned, they prayed for their tormentors. Though, for the most part, impoverished in worldly goods, they gave freely of what they had to brethren in need. They were considered by sophisticated standards to be uneducated and ignorant men, yet people could not cope with the wisdom and the Spirit by which they spoke (Acts 4:8–12; 6:10; 2:6; cf. Matt. 10:19, 20; Mark 13:11; Luke 12:12). Something about them was different. There was a shine on their faces; a sparkle in their eyes. Just by looking at them one could tell that "they had been with Jesus" (Acts 4:13). No wonder they came to be called *Christians,* for their lives reflected His character (Acts 11:26).[15]

What is also evident, these early believers were doing the works of Christ, as He had said (John 14:12). All the characteristics of Jesus' ministry are seen in them, and in the fruitfulness of the harvest, there was even a "greater work." Beginning with the ingathering of 3,000 at Pentecost, the out-

---

[15] It is interesting that the word *Christian* literally means "belonging to Christ." The name of Christ is a substantive from the Greek language, meaning "the anointed one," while the adjectival ending *ian* comes from the Latin *iani,* meaning "belonging to." Closely akin to this term is the word *saint,* meaning "one who is set apart or owned by God," and in this sense, every Christian is holy.

reach accelerated daily, until within a generation the Gospel penetrated large segments of the civilized world, and the work was going forward unabated when the Acts of the Apostles closed (Acts 28:31). In fact, the Acts really has no conclusion, for we are still living in that harvest age of the Spirit, and it will continue until the great commission is fulfilled.[16]

Is this not the way Jesus planned it? He did not come Himself to evangelize the world, but to make it possible for the world to be saved. Most of His time on earth was spent training some disciples for the task. When this was done, after offering the necessary sacrifice, He soon returned to heaven. The work of announcing the Good News was committed to His Church. He knew that they would carry on, for the Comforter would come to manifest His Power in and through their witness.

Receiving the Gift

His indwelling Presence is the great gift which Christ promises to His people (John 14:16, 17). The Spirit is given, not by virtue of any merit in man, but simply because God delights to give the best to His children, and the best He knows is Himself. Jesus reminds His disciples that if an earthly father, being evil, knows how to give good gifts unto his children, "how much more shall your heavenly Father give the Holy Spirit to them that ask him" (Luke 11:13).

The gift comes with the asking. No striving to be worthy is needed, since every provision has already been made by the Father. Man can only believe what God says He will do, and act accordingly. Jesus assures that "For everyone who asks receives; he who seeks finds; and to him who knocks, the door will be opened" (Luke 11:10 NIV). The life of faith is so incredibly uncomplicated that the self-righteous person invariably misses it. For receiving Christ implies a renunciation of human sufficiency in all its varied forms, and a total reliance

---

[16] Deserving of special note in reference to the witness-bearing function of the Comforter is Harry Boer, *Pentecost and Missions* (Grand Rapids: Wm. B. Eerdmans, 1961), a study originally submitted as a doctrinal dissertation at the Free University in Amsterdam (1955). The author convincingly shows that the great commission derives its meaning and power from the Pentecostal outpouring.

upon the efficacy of God's redeeming grace. It is to live as a child in total dependence upon the loving Father, confident that whatever He does is good, and that He is able to take care of every need.

Where un-Christlikeness is recognized, of course, it must be confessed, which means to agree with the truth. Man cannot argue with the Spirit and expect His blessing. To enjoy His fellowship there must be a willingness to walk in the light of God's Word. As new insight to Christ's holiness is given, so there grows a deeper realization of sin's residue in the flesh, accompanied by an intensifying desire to be like the Master. This sensitizing of the conscience does not imply condemnation; but it does urge constant vigilance against sin, and continuous appropriation of the victorious life of Christ.[17] The obedient Christian always lives triumphantly, "free from the law of sin and death". (Rom. 8:2).

Our Need Today

Living in the fulness of the Holy Spirit is as much the privilege of Christ's followers today as of those first disciples who tarried in the upper room. The promise is not a dogma to be argued, but a reality to be experienced. Nor is it a fringe benefit for a few Christian zealots, or the peculiar teaching of some evangelical churches. True, it may be called by different names and variously interpreted according to one's doctrinal viewpoint, but the reality of the all-encompassing, Christ-

---

[17] What is said here applies to any evangelical understanding of sanctification, though, depending upon the way sin is defined, some will make more of the crisis element in dealing with the carnal nature. This would be the case with those who distinguish between involuntary perversion in humanity and willful transgression. Such a differentiation, however precarious, allows for a definite cleansing of conscious sin when the problem is faced, including self-centeredness. On the other hand, those who see any deviation from God's absolute nature as sin, whether understood or not, would naturally hesitate to speak of full sanctification at any point in this life. Nevertheless, the desire for holiness can be just as intense, and as long as the sin nature is reckoned dead, the fully consecrated soul through the blood of Christ lives victorious over sin. This is the point which I am stressing. The Christian, whatever his doctrinal point of view, should always be fully given to God.

possessing holiness of the Spirit is basic New Testament Christianity.

We may obscure the enduring significance of Pentecost by undue attention to the wind and fire and tongues associated with the initial outpouring (Acts 2:1–13). While these phenomena dramatized the event, they were not what changed the lives of the waiting disciples, nor are they given much prominence thereafter. The abiding value of Pentecost appears in the daily, ongoing witness of those early Christians. Again and again, they are said to be filled with the Spirit (Acts 4:8, 31; 6:3, 5; 7:55; 9:17; 11:24; 13:9, 52). Not that they always maintained this walk, but it was their privilege. That being filled with the Spirit was considered the norm of Christian experience is evident from Paul's Letter to the Ephesians, when using an imperative, he commands the Church to continuously abound in this state (Eph. 5:18).

To the degree that we take this to heart, and permit the Spirit to enthrone Christ in our lives, we can expect to do His bidding. Without the energizing power of God we are as useless as light bulbs without electricity. Make no mistake about it, making men whole is the Spirit's work. Being a supernatural ministry, it cannot be engineered by man. Human effort can organize campaigns, publish literature, raise budgets, build edifices, earn degrees, and even civilize nations; but only God can breathe into a soul the breath of life.

The secret of the Incarnation lies for us here. As we open ourselves fully to Him who gave life to the Son, and who raises up His Church, we may be sure that Christ will continue His ministry through us.

This is how you should pray . . . .
Matthew 6:9 NIV

2
His Communion Through Prayer

The Spirit imparts the divine nature, but it is sustained through prayer. In this holy communion faith experiences its highest privilege and greatest power. Prayer's prominence in the life of Jesus offers another insight to the dynamic quality of His ministry.

The Praying Son

Prayer shines through the Gospels like a dominant color in a painting, giving the whole picture of Christ a characteristic hue.[1] This practice is particularly noticed during crucial moments in His redemptive mission—His baptism (Luke 3:21, 22), the selection of the twelve apostles (Luke 6:12, 13), the confession of His Messiahship (Luke 9:18), the transfiguration experience on the mount (Luke 9:28, 29), while contemplating His impending death (John 12:27, 28), the last supper (Matt.

---

[1] The subject receives notice, in varying degrees, in most standard histories of Christ and New Testament theologies. There are also any number of special studies, of which the most complete is probably James G. S. S. Thomson, *The Praying Christ* (Grand Rapids: Wm. B. Eerdmans, 1959). Other helpful volumes are by Andrew Murray, *With Christ in the School of Prayer* (Chicago: M. A. Donahue and Co., n.d.); Elton Trueblood, *The Lord's Prayers* (New York: Harper and Row, 1965); David M. M'Intyre, *The Prayer Life of Our Lord* (London: Morgan and Scott, n.d.); Lewis Maclachlan, *The Teaching of Jesus on Prayer* (London: James Clark and Co., 1958); and Ray C. Stedman, *Jesus Teaches on Prayer* (Waco: Word, 1975). Shorter treatments are by N. N. Ronning, *Jesus in Prayer* (Minneapolis: Augsburg Publishing House, 1931); John Henry Strong, *Jesus the Man of Prayer* (Philadelphia: Judson, 1945); Fred L. Fisher, *Prayer in the New Testament* (Philadelphia: Westminster, 1954); Ralph Spaulding Cushman, *The Prayers of Jesus* (New York: Abingdon, 1955); among others.

26:27), the travail of His soul in Gethsemane (Matt. 26:39–46; Mark 14:32–34; Luke 22:39–46), and finally, the agony of the cross (Luke 22:32; 23:46). The decisions faced on these occasions produced a dependence and affirmation which could only find expression in prayer.

The Gospels also disclose the Master praying as He prepared Himself for the demands of His preaching ministry (Mark 1:35, 38; Luke 5:16). Prayer is noted, too, when little children were brought to Him for His blessing (Mark 10:16). It is also associated with His miraculous power, as when He healed the multitudes (Mark 1:35); fed the five thousand (Mark 6:41; Matt. 14:19; Luke 9:16; John 6:11); and later fed the four thousand (Mark 8:6; Matt. 15:36); healed the deaf mute (Mark 7:34); and raised Lazarus from the dead (John 11:41).

Significantly, the disciples knew Christ was praying in each of these instances. They could see the priority of prayer in His life; and knew if they were to follow Him, they would have to live by the same rule. It was this knowledge which led them to ask the Master to teach them to pray (Luke 11:1). Not surprisingly, frequent biblical reference is made to Christ's prayers in connection with the disciples' own experiences. He was praying on the mountain when He saw them at sea in distress (Mark 6:46); prayers of thanksgiving were offered when He sent out the disciples two by two (Matt. 11:25, 26; cf. Luke 10:21); and upon their return with reports of God's blessing (Luke 10:21, 22). The same gladness resounded as He broke bread in the house of the two disciples at Emmaus (Luke 24:30); and at His last farewell before the ascension into heaven (Luke 24:50, 51). The greatest example, of course, is His High Priestly prayer, which focuses upon the eleven disciples (John 17:6–19). Interestingly, in the only place where Jesus spoke of His own prayer life, it concerned His love for Peter (Luke 22:31, 32).

A Regular Habit

The variety of these references to prayer—during all kinds of circumstances, at different times and places, in matters great and small—suggests an habitual attitude. As James

G. S. S. Thomson concluded: "Prayer was the atmosphere in which He lived; it was the air that He breathed." [2]

Accenting this spontaneous life of prayer were regular periods set aside for uninterrupted communion, probably three times a day.[3] Mention is made that "in the early morning, while it was still dark, He arose and went out and departed to a lonely place, and was praying there" (Mark 1:35 NASB). Again it is said that as the multitude clamored for attention, He "often withdrew to lonely places and prayed" (Luke 5:16 NIV), indicating that there were many places and many occasions when Jesus went away to pray. This was a habit of His life.

Physical exertion could not deter Him from these seasons of spiritual renewal. After working all day He would sometimes slip off and spend the night in prayer (Luke 6:12; Mark 6:45–48; Matt. 14:22, 23; John 6:14, 15). Even when He was so busy ministering to people during the day that He "had no leisure so much as to eat," Jesus still took time to pray (Mark 6:31, 46). He could get along without food, but He could not live without prayer.[4] Other things were necessary, but prayer was in-

---

[2] Op. cit., p. 36. Dr. Thomson observes that the translation of Psalms 109:4, "But I am prayer" or "But I am a Prayer," was literally true of Christ.

[3] As a devout member of the Jewish community, it is likely that Jesus faithfully observed the custom of praying in the morning at the time of the burnt offering in the Temple; in the afternoon when the daily sacrifice was offered as the trumpets sounded; and in the evening at sunset when the Temple gates were closed. The practice began centuries before Christ's day (Dan. 6:11, 14), probably going back to the practice of reciting the Shema in the morning and evening (Deut. 11:19). By New Testament times it seems to have become a general rule in Judaism, and was continued by the early Church (cf. Acts 3:1; 10:3, 30). Jesus by no means limited His praying to these set times, nor was He bound by any liturgical formula; nevertheless, these established periods provided a fabric of discipline to His devotion. A well-documented study of "Daily Prayer in the Life of Jesus and the Primitive Church" is by Joachim Jeremias, in the Studies in Biblical Theology series, *The Prayers of Jesus* (Naperville, Ill.: Alec R. Allenson, Inc., 1966), pp. 66–81.

[4] The practice of forgoing food when spiritual needs were more urgent seems to have been well established in Jesus' ministry. Sometimes, as in the above instance, and when speaking to the woman at the well (John 4:31–34), abstinence from food was occasioned by the

dispensable. No other activity could substitute for this discipline of His soul. Prayer was His way of getting things done. He never got behind in His work because He never got behind in prayer.

Content of His Prayers

The words of Jesus' prayers are recorded on nine occasions. Though generally brief, these excerpts and summations permit an intimate view into His mind.[5] The first occurred as He reflected upon the lack of spiritual perception of the inhabitants of Bethsaida and Capernaum, where so many of His miracles were manifest. Seeing around Him the few disciples who had believed, Jesus uttered in jubilation: "I thank thee, Father, Lord of heaven and earth, that thou hast hidden these things from the wise and understanding and revealed them to babes; yea, Father, for such was thy gracious will" (Matt. 11:25, 26 RSV). He then spoke of the fellowship He knew with

---

demands of the Kingdom work (cf. Mark 8:1–3). At other times, He deliberately observed periods of fasting in order to give Himself fully to prayer and reflection. Such was the case for forty days as He embarked on His public ministry (Matt. 4:1, 2; Luke 4:2; Mark 1:12, 13). Though this discipline was not given much attention in the Gospels thereafter, apparently fasting and prayer was a part of His practice, since He urged it upon His disciples (Matt. 17:21; Mark 9:29). Whether or not He fasted twice a week, like the Pharisees, is not stated, although in pointing out the abuse of the custom, His language, "*when* you fast," assumes that His disciples observed some kind of ritual (Matt. 6:16). That they did not have the works of austerity which typified the Pharisees, as well as the followers of John the Baptist (Mark 2:18), seems clear. However, Jesus assured them that fasting should be taken more seriously after He was gone (Mark 2:20).

[5] I am aware of critics who disprove of this attempt, like D. Rudolf Bultmann, who says that it is a "great mistake to discuss the prayer life of Jesus," since this would put man "in the place of God": *Jesus and the Word* (New York: Charles Scribner's Sons, 1934), pp. 188, 189. Granted our limited ability to interpret a spiritual conversation, still the words of Christ's prayers are as much a part of the revelation as anything else in the Bible, and probably no other aspect of His life casts more light upon those things most dear to Him. If one feels a need to consider the problems of higher criticism in these prayers, a helpful summary may be found in A. Raymond George, *Communion with God in the New Testament* (London: The Epworth Press, 1953), especially pp. 31–92, 197–206.

the Father, acknowledging His sovereignty in the way ordinary people were raised up to follow Him (Matt. 11:27). Virtually an identical prayer was heard later as the seventy disciples return from an evangelistic excursion and Jesus "rejoiced in the Holy Spirit" (Luke 10:21–23 RSV).[6]

Joyous confidence in His communion with God emerged again in His prayer at the grave of Lazarus: Lifting up His eyes,[7] Jesus said, "Father, I thank Thee that Thou heardest Me. And I knew that Thou hearest me always; but because of the people standing around I said it, that they may believe that Thou didst send Me" (John 11:41, 42 NASB). His desire was that the raising of the dead man, already assured "for the glory of God" (John 11:4), would cause the onlookers to recognize the divine source and direction of His mission.

When Jesus discussed the nearness of His death with the Greeks, He felt the natural inclination to take a different course. Suddenly, He addressed an unseen but very present Person: "Now my heart is troubled, and what shall I say? 'Father, save me from this hour'? No, it was for this very reason I came to this hour. Father, glorify your name!" (John 12:27, 28 NIV). This interjected dialogue with the Father expressed anew His consuming desire that, come what may, God be glorified in the fulfillment of His will. This attitude is again apparent in Gethsemane on the eve of His crucifixion, when He cries: "O my Father, if it be possible, let this cup pass from me; nevertheless not as I will, but as thou wilt" (Matt. 26:39; cf. Mark 14:36; Luke 22:42). Whatever the cost, He knows that nothing must hinder God's plan for His life.

Three times Jesus prayed on the cross. Once He asked the Father to forgive those who caused His suffering (Luke 23:34), showing in the prayer His identification with the God of all

---

[6] Since the return of the seventy disciples is not recorded by Matthew, possibly this prayer was included with his account of the return of the twelve (Mark 6:30; Luke 9:10). The prayers, however, could have easily been repeated, since the occasions are analogous.

[7] It might be noted from this reference that Jesus was standing when He prayed. This was the case also in John 17:1. However, on another occasion He knelt (Luke 22:41); and in Gethsemane He "fell on His face" (Matt. 26:39). At other times He may have been sitting in a relaxed position. From this we can reasonably infer that posture in prayer is something determined by the occasion, and it has nothing to do with the spirit of prayer.

grace. Again, in the depth of His agony, sensing the remorse of being forsaken, He utters the cry of dereliction, "Eloi, Eloi, lama sabachthani?" (Mark 15:34; cf. Matt. 27:46). It would seem that for a moment, in His human consciousness, He felt that God had turned His back upon Him. But that there was no wavering in His trust is apparent in His last prayer, framed in the words of the Psalmist: "Father, into thy hands I commend my spirit" (Luke 23:46; cf. Ps. 31:5). He knew that He had been faithful, and in the confidence of perfect filial love, He rested Himself in God.

Our High Priest

The most extensive information we have regarding the way Jesus prayed comes in His consecration on the eve of the Crucifixion (John 17:1–26). Constituting a conclusion to the farewell discourse in the upper room (John 13:1—16:33), it sealed what had been said to the disciples, and bound His earthly ministry with that which was to follow in the coming of the Comforter. From the standpoint of His own Person and office, it is the purest revelation of the mind of Christ in Scripture.[8]

---

[8] I concur with Melanchthon, when he remarked shortly before His death: "There is no voice which has ever been heard, either in heaven or in earth, more exalted, more holy, more fruitful, more sublime, than this prayer offered up by the Son of God Himself," quoted in Marcus Dods, *The Gospel of St. John*, Vol. 2 (New York: A. C. Armstrong and Son, 1892), p. 248. Whether or not others share this opinion, few passages offer greater reward for serious study. For those seeking more insight, standard commentaries will be helpful. Those which I have consulted with profit include Bengel, Calvin, Luther, Westcott, Meyer, Dods, Lange, Clark, Henry, Turner, Plummer (Cambridge), Blaney (Wesleyan), and Hull (Broadman). There are also a number of volumes given entirely to this chapter, of which Marcus Rainsford, *Our Lord Prays for His Own* (Chicago: Moody, n.d.) is probably best known. Also of importance, though less exhaustive, are the writings of Charles Ross, *The Inner Sanctuary* (London: The Banner of Truth Trust, 1967 © 1888), pp. 199–247; Thomas Dehany Bernard, *The Central Teaching of Jesus Christ* (London: Macmillan and Co., 1892), pp. 329–416; Henry Barclay Sweete, *The Last Discourse and Prayer of Our Lord* (London: Macmillan and Co., 1914), pp. 159–187; and the little book by Alva Ross Brown, *Our Lord's Most Sublime Words* (Kingsport: Southern Publishers, 1930).

The prayer falls into three parts, following the sacrificial pattern of Israel's high priest on the Day of Atonement.[9] Jesus first offered Himself to God (17:1–5); then His disciples (17:6–19); and finally the entire Church (17:20–26). The divisions show the logical progression of His mission, beginning with His own work, extending Himself to the few apostles, and through them ultimately reaching the world. Woven through it all, unifying the whole, is His passion for the glory of God in the salvation of men.

His petition for Himself is that the Father may be glorified in the Son, and that they share together in the ensuing triumph of His grace. "Father, the hour is come; glorify thy Son, that thy Son also may glorify thee" (vs. 1). God had established Christ's authority over all men to give eternal life, and Jesus had been faithful to His mandate (vss. 2, 3). Through His finished work on the cross, Jesus knew that He would be glorified in that splendor which was His "before the world was" (vss. 4, 5).[10]

Having affirmed His sense of God's purpose, our High Priest turned His attention to those particular eleven men whom God had given Him. Most of Christ's active ministry centered around these disciples. They were the Father's love gift to the Son to whom He had revealed His inmost Self. With the tenderness of a loving parent entrusted with children by God, He confessed how precious they were in His sight (vss. 6–8): "I pray not for the world, but for them which thou hast

---

[9] It was the practice of the high priest on this occasion to make an atonement for himself and his house (Lev. 16:6), after which he did the same for the priesthood, and, finally, for all the people of the Covenant community (Lev. 16:33). This has led commentators to refer to John 17 as "The High Priestly Prayer," noting the priestly role assumed by Jesus (e.g., 17:19), though kingly and prophetic elements are also present. However, some prefer to speak of it as "The Lord's Prayer," as distinguished from the passage usually called by that name. Others designate it as "The Prayer of Consecration" or "The Intercession of Christ."

[10] It is wonderful how Jesus could speak of His work as having already been finished, though, in fact, He had not yet died on the cross (cf. Luke 9:28–31). What appears to be a contradiction, however, offers no problem when it is remembered that Jesus could visualize the eternal will of God. Reflecting upon this heavenly reality seems natural in prayer.

given me; for they are thine. And all mine are thine, and thine
are mine; and I am glorified in them" (vss. 9, 10). Soon Jesus
would leave them, and realizing that they must carry on His
work, He asked the Father to keep them from the snares of the
evil one (vss. 11–16), and to sanctify them through the truth
(vss. 17–19). There was a note of urgency in His voice, for He
knew that unless the disciples fulfilled His trust, the world
would never know the Gospel.

Then, declaring His faith, He lifted His vision beyond the
Eleven, and prayed for the untold multitudes who would
come to believe on Him "through their word" (vs. 20). There
is an extent in this entreaty which reached to the ends of the
earth, and still embraces every unborn child in His compassion. Looking to this emerging Church, He besought the
Father that "all may be one" in divine fellowship, and "that
the world may believe that thou hast sent me" (vs. 21). Finally, projecting His mind to the end of the age, and the glory
that was His with the Father, He prayed that the whole universal Church of believers be with Him forever in God's eternal love (vss. 22, 24). Reflecting again upon His mission, He
closed by reminding the Father of His great desire: "that the
love wherewith thou hast loved me may be in them, and I in
them" (vss. 25, 26).

His Human Dependence

If Jesus was God, why did He have to pray? The answer to
this lies in acknowledging the human component of His personality. As a man, He knew that He could not live by bread
alone. He had to renew His strength by waiting upon the
Spirit. The pressures of the alien world only made Him more
conscious of the need to abide in the secret place of the Most
High.

Thus, prayer was our Lord's way of expressing His total
dependence upon God. He realized that He did not work
alone, nor did He speak in His own wisdom. All that He did
and said was in the power of Him who sent Him. Prayer was
an affirmation of this confidence; the assurance that His soul
was in absolute alignment with the mind of the Father, not by
passive resignation but in active conformity to His purpose.

The certainty of God's will being done filled His life with
thanksgiving and praise, and this spirit dominated His prayers
(Matt. 15:36; 26:27; Mark 14:23; Luke 10:21; John 6:11; 11:41,
42; 17:1–26). Even on the way to Gethsemane Jesus sang a
hymn and gave thanks (Mark 14:26).[11] This gladness reflected
the atmosphere of heaven, with which His soul was in constant communion.[12]

When He reached out in love to lift up others, His supplications took on the dimension of intercession (John 11:15;
17:6–26; Luke 22:32; 23:34; Mark 10:16). Being vicarious,
such prayers were not easy. Sometimes they resembled the
sacrifices offered by the priesthood on the altar of the Temple,
with strenuous, exhausting, heartrending labor on behalf of
those represented. In Gethsemane His burden was so heavy
that while He prayed "his sweat was as it were great drops of
blood falling down to the ground" (Luke 22:44). Prayer was
indeed the sweat and tears of His ministry (Heb. 5:7). The
battle of the cross was fought and won on His knees.

Through all Christ's praying is the beautiful sense of His
oneness with the Father. Prayer to Him was communion
within the Trinity. Nothing gave Him more delight than the
contemplation of Their fellowship and glory. It was during
prayer on the Mount that His countenance was transfigured
and His garments appeared as shining light; on another occasion while He prayed the heavens opened and the Spirit
mightily descended upon Him. Little wonder that John wrote
of seeing His glory, "the glory of the one and only Son, who
came from the Father" (John 1:14 NIV). He had seen the Master pray.

---

[11] The hymn on this occasion would have been the second part of
the Hallel, Psalms 115–118, which was sung by Jews after the Passover meal was finished. These psalms accentuate the will of God to
bring His people to redemption through His sacrifice. They ring with
praise. Reading them in the light of Calvary gives the hymn sung by
Jesus an indescribable wonder. A brief description of the custom is in
my book *Written in Blood* (Old Tappan, N.J.: Fleming H. Revell,
1972), pp. 68–71.

[12] Joachim Jeremias notes that "thanksgiving is one of the foremost
characteristics of the new age." So Jesus' practice is not just a custom;
rather He is "actualizing God's reign here and now." *The Prayers of
Jesus*, p. 78.

Teaching on Fatherhood

Jesus introduced in His prayers a significant new intimacy with God which far surpassed anything assumed in Judaism. Though the concept of God's fatherhood appears in the Old Testament, never before is the Father-child relationship placed in such tenderness and trust. The Aramaic word *Abba* (Mark 14:36) was probably the original term used by Jesus in all the instances in which the Father was addressed.[13] It conveys the idea of familiarity, the kind of chatter a child would use in speaking of his "daddy." No Jew would have adopted this everyday language in addressing the Almighty. It would have been considered disrespectful. For Jesus to disregard custom in this manner displays the attitude of filial trust at the heart of His prayer life.

Jesus teaches us to pray after the same manner, of which the model given to the disciples sets the pattern (Matt. 6:9–13; Luke 11:2–4).[14] The invocation, "Our Father," assumes that

---

[13] Since almost certainly Jesus spoke Aramaic, the people's language, ἀββά would have been the word used, though only in Mark 14:36 is the actual Aramaic term recorded. Kittel, op. cit., I, p. 6. A thorough discussion of this whole concept may be found in Joachim Jeremias, *The Prayers of Jesus*, pp. 11–65, 82–115.

[14] The prayer appears to have been given on two different occasions, with slight variations: first, in the Sermon on the Mount, while Jesus was teaching the disciples to avoid pretense and vain repetition; and later, in response to the disciples' request that He teach them to pray. Though not intended to be recited as a mere formality, the few sentences enunciate many profound truths about prayer, and when uttered with understanding, bring a child of God into harmony with the supplications of Jesus. We can appreciate why so many authors, representing different perspectives and gifts, have written whole books on the prayer, among them Marcus Dods, Joachim Jeremias, John Lowe, Georges Cardinal Grente, Norman K. Elliott, Ernest Lohmeyer, Roger Hicks, Walter Lüthi, Hugh Martin, Evelyn Underhill, M. Angeline Bouchard, George C. Baldwin, Helmut Thieliche, Anthony C. Deane, Frederic W. Farrow, H. N. Grimley, J. D. Jones, Alan Redpath, E. M. Blacklock, J. C. Macaulay, and even an Unknown Christian. This partial listing suggests the extent of resources available. If I were to turn to only a few volumes, the selection would surely include Thomas Watson, *The Lord's Prayer* (London: The Banner of Truth Trust, 1965 © 1692); W. Denton, *A Commentary on the Lord's Prayer* (New York: Carlton and Porter, 1865); Newman Hall, *The Lord's Prayer* (Edinburgh: T. & T. Clark, 1883); and G. A. Studdert-Kennedy, *The Wicket Gate* (London: Hodder and Stoughton, 1923).

the interests of God and man are inseparable.[15] That He would instruct the Church to think this way underscores the new kind of family relationship which He opened to all who have His Spirit in their hearts (cf. Gal. 4:6; Rom. 8:15, 16; 2 Cor. 6:15).

In this childlike confidence and simplicity, the disciples were taught to live in loving dependence upon their heavenly Father (Matt. 6:1–7; 23:14; Mark 12:38–40; Luke 20:47). Prayer is the means by which they were to expect their daily necessities (Matt. 6:11; Luke 11:3); find deliverance from temptation (Matt. 6:13; Luke 11:4; cf. Matt. 26:41; Mark 14:38; Luke 22:40, 46); have protection in times of calamity (Matt. 24:20; cf. 8:26); and, above all, receive the indwelling Spirit of Christ (Luke 11:13). It is not that God must hear our requests before He can answer, for He knows what we need before we ask (Matt. 6:8, 32). Rather prayer puts man in the position to receive what God desires to give.

The secret is to want what God wants—to "seek first his kingdom and his righteousness" (Matt. 6:33 RSV). Hence, Jesus stressed that the primary burden of prayer is not that human needs be supplied, but that God's Name be hallowed, His Kingdom come, and His will be done on earth as it is in heaven (Matt. 6:10; Luke 11:2). Only in the context of Him to whom belongs glory forever can humanity know fulfillment (Matt. 6:11).

In His Name

The power of prayer is the Name of Christ. "Whatsoever ye shall ask in my name, that will I do . . ." (John 14:13; cf. 15:16; 16:23–26). The Name of Jesus, of course, is just another way of expressing the Person and work of the Master. To pray in His Name is to pray in the character of Christ, in His mind frame, that is, to pray as He Himself would pray in our situation, and, indeed, as He is praying now as our Mediator in heaven (Heb. 9:24; cf. 1 John 2:1). Sensitivity to the Spirit of

---

[15] Note how discriminating Jesus is in His use of the pronoun. Never does He refer to "our Father" in His own prayers. Moreover, He always distinguishes between "My Father" and "your Father" in what He says to others. Altogether the Lord speaks of God as Father 170 times in the Gospels, of which 21, including parallels, pertain to His personal address to God.

Christ and obedience to His truth is indispensable to such praying. Only then does He promise to answer, "that the Father may be glorified in the Son" (John 14:13).

This demands that we carefully examine our lives in the light of Christ's nature and purpose. We cannot pray in His Name unless we abide in Him, and His words in us (John 15:7). Anything unbecoming His likeness will hinder communion: pride (Luke 18:10–14), greed (Mark 12:40; Luke 20:47), an unforgiving spirit (Matt. 6:13–14; 18:21–35; Mark 11:25), disharmony with other worshipers (Matt. 18:19), even the attempt to appear pious (Matt. 6:1–7; 23:14; Mark 12:38–40; Luke 20:47). Where there is conscious sin, the first step in prayer is to confess that we are not in the Name of Christ, and to make things right. Such honest heart-searching is not easy, but it is the only way to know the fellowship of Christ. This becomes apparent when one enters the Kingdom. But its implications, scarcely perceived in the beginning, have deepening meaning as we walk with Him. The experience of holiness grows in proportion to the experience of prayer.

Within this context, nothing is impossible. Jesus declares boldly: "All things, whatsoever you shall ask in prayer, believing, ye shall receive" (Matt. 21:22; cf. 17:18–21; Mark 9:29; 11:23, 24; Luke 11:9). Such certainty shatters so much of our devotional exercise we call prayer. We may even think that it is presumptuous to believe that God grants what we ask. After all, we reason, isn't communion with Christ the most precious gift? And in the last analysis, doesn't only God know what is best for us?

This notion may reflect a commendable sense of modesty in the petitioner, but strangely, it is not stressed by Christ. To the contrary, Jesus taught His disciples to live in the assurance of answered prayer, and to ask until they received (Matt. 7:7–11; Luke 11:5–10; 18:1–8). Persistence is necessary, not that God is unwilling to respond, but that resistance in the one praying might be overcome. Undue anxiety about the answer might itself indicate a lack of faith in God's will and love.

Fellowship with Christ is thus the means of obtaining His blessing through prayer, and the answer the confirmation of our will in union with His. This is not to say that all prayer will be answered immediately, for He may want to teach us greater trust and patience in the delay. Nor are we to assume that the answer will come exactly as we envision. The heavenly Father may grant the request according to some higher dimension of need. But when we live in His Spirit, what we ask He will do, because we are doing what He asks. Prayer is simply believing God to supply what is needed to fulfill His will. In this sense, it is divinely initiated; we are but a channel through which the Spirit of Jesus offers His supplications.

The Method of Harvest

Thus assured, the disciples were sent forth as ministering servants of Christ. When they were put down for their witness, they were not to fret or try to retaliate, but to pray for those who despitefully used them (Matt. 5:44; cf. Luke 6:28). When confronting forces of evil that bind the hearts and minds of men, prayer was their way of bringing deliverance (Mark 9:14–29). When they looked out upon the teeming multitudes of lost people, without love or direction, Jesus made emphatic their course of action: "Pray ye therefore the Lord of the harvest, that he will send forth labourers into his harvest" (Matt. 9:38; cf. Luke 10:2).

Everything else revolved around their practice of this command. The superhuman task to which they were called required a supernatural provision. That resource was prayer. Through it the Spirit could perform through them the same mighty works that Christ had done in their midst, and even "greater works than these" (John 14:12–14).

To this end, the disciples were ordained to "go and bring forth fruit"—fruit that would remain and grow. As Jesus said, ". . . whatsoever ye shall ask of the Father in my name, he may give it you" (John 15:16). Fruitfulness is here a condition as well as a consequence of prayer. Barrenness bespeaks lifelessness. Unless there is continuing reproduction of those things dear to Christ, how can one be in vital communion with His Spirit? Yet conversely, where there is effectual prayer—that kind of supplication which enters into the very life stream of God—the manifestations of the Son's work inevitably follow.

Here is evangelism in its most basic expression. To paraphrase the words of Dr. Lewis Sperry Chafer, "Winning men is more a work of pleading for souls than a service of pleading with them." [16] It is in the closet of intercession where the victory is won. Any activity not issuing from this discipline is an exercise in futility. Better to master this lesson in the school of Christ than to achieve excellence in all the arts of persuasion. The eloquent speaker may influence men, but only a man of prayer can influence God.

C. H. Spurgeon could have been speaking to us when he advised his students: "The more familiar you are with the court of heaven, the better shall you discharge your heavenly trust." [17] Or to put it in the words of Bernard of Clairvaux, writing to a young priest:

> Take heed to give your words the voice of power. What is that do you ask? It is that your works harmonize with your words, or rather that your words with your works, that you be careful to do before you teach. It is a most salutary order of things that you should first bear the burden you place on others, and learn from yourself how men should be ruled . . . . Understand, to the quieting of your conscience, that in these two commandments, that is, of precept and example, the whole of your duty resides. You, however, if you be wise, will add yet a third, namely, a zeal for prayer to complete that treble repetition of the Gospel concerning feeding the sheep. You will then know that no sacrament of that trinity is in any wise broken by you, if you feed them by word, by example, and by the fruit of holy prayers. Now abideth speech, example, prayer, these three; but the greatest of these is prayer. For although, as it has been said, the strength of speech is work, yet prayer wins grace and efficacy for both work and speech. [18]

---

[16] Lewis Sperry Chafer, *True Evangelism* (London: Marshall, Morgan and Scott, 1919), p. 93.

[17] C. H. Spurgeon, *Lectures to My Students* (London: Marshall, Morgan and Scott, 1954), p. 43.

[18] Bernard of Clairvaux, quoted in Jane Stoddart, *Private Prayer in Christian Story* (London: Hodder and Stoughton, 1927), pp. 65, 66.

The Pathway of Power

By example and by teaching, Jesus shows us what this means—individually and corporately; secretly and publicly; in special appointments and with a continuous attitude—fulfilling His mission is supremely a life of prayer, a life totally given to God. Now through His present mediation for us before the Father, and His Spirit indwelling our hearts, He places this vocation before every Christian.

Yet, like those first disciples, we are so slow to follow His way. Though they were continually exposed to His praying, and had even asked for special help in learning how, still for a long time they did not appear to have internalized the imperative nature of prayer. There is no record that they spent long hours in unhurried communion on their own. Sometimes Jesus took a few with Him when He went up on the mountain, but they didn't seem to know what to do when they got there. At His transfiguration, rather than talk with Moses and Elijah about His sacrifice, they wanted to build three tabernacles to commemorate the event. In Gethsemane, as Jesus agonized over the cross, the weary Peter, James, and John fell off to sleep. And on those occasions when the disciples made requests of Jesus, somewhat analogous to prayer, they usually asked amiss, indicating that they did not really understand the burden of their Lord (e.g., Matt. 14:28; 15:23; 20:22; John 4:31; 9:2, 3).

Why they did not develop more discipline in their own practice of prayer is not explained. Perhaps they were simply disposed to let Jesus do the praying for them. Or was it that they had not yet entered sufficiently into spiritual reality to see their need of it? Whatever the reason, in the Resurrection appearance of Jesus, His breathing upon them may have been more than a foretaste of the Spirit's outpouring (John 20:22). It may have instilled within them a new spiritual awareness of prayer.

In any event, the disciples seem to sense its necessity thereafter (Acts 1:14). In this attitude they experience the fulness of the Spirit, and as they go forth in the love and power of

Pentecost, they cease not calling upon the Name of the Lord. The Book of Acts literally pulsates with prayer.[19]

Our Upper Room

Just as they learned Christ's secret strength, so must we. We can get along without some things, but we cannot live without prayer. Without this vital energy of the Spirit, we are as lifeless as a body without breath.

To pray without ceasing is thus the rule of life. Whenever this communion is broken, we must find out why, and make correction. If the problem is sin, it must be dealt with immediately. Prayer makes us live in conformity to Christ, not in mere submission, but in joyous affirmation of His will.

As we enter into His intercessions for a lost world, we are brought to examine our motives for evangelism, for we cannot pray for a person we do not love, nor love one we do not want to serve. If ever we are honest about our ministry, surely it is when we meet with God in the inner sanctuary of our heart. Here is our upper room, where we can commune with the precious Spirit, receive His cleansing, offer up our supplications, and in the renewing of His strength, go forth to do exploits for our loving Saviour.

---

[19] Prayer is given more prominence in the Acts than in any other book of the Bible. Altogether there are 31 specific references to prayer in the book (by contrast, Luke has 30 references to divine entreaty, and Matthew follows with 20). In the verb forms, the tenses emphasize action and progress, as related to the whole life of the Church. Prayer is not some distant goal which they are striving to reach; rather it is a very real and present fact of their experience. When the noun form occurs, it is used in all four cases, and in both the singular and plural, indicating its general practice, privately and collectively. They prayed in various places—homes, on housetops, jails, the Temple, seashore, on board ships; at different hours of the day; and in all kinds of situations—when facing physical danger, when in need of guidance or spiritual power, when commissioning persons for service, when departing from friends, when concerned about others' needs, when offering thanks, and when facing death. It seemed they were ready to pray anywhere, anytime, and under any conditions. And what is most remarkable, all their prayers seem to have been answered.

This that is written must yet be accomplished in me.

Luke 22:37

•

3

His Word of Authority

Whether he was praying to the Father or speaking to men, Jesus lived by the Word of God. The consciousness of this infallible guide gave direction and power to His life. In this fact we see one more reason for His extraordinary witness.

Imbued with Scripture

The Old Testament Scriptures, which every Israelite regarded as Holy Writ, constituted the basis of Jesus' education.[1] In keeping with the commandments of Moses, He started to learn these sacred writings at His parents' knees (Deut. 4:9; 6:6, 7; 11:18–21; 31:12, 13). Later when He attended the compulsory synagogue school at Nazareth, He systematically studied the law and the prophets, along with their accepted interpretations by the Jewish fathers.[2] In addition,

---

[1] The Old Testament canon as we know it today was well established by the time of Christ. A concise and competent discussion of the Jewish canon of Scripture may be found in R. K. Harrison, *Introduction to the Old Testament* (Grand Rapids: Wm. B. Eerdmans, 1969), pp. 211–288; and F. F. Bruce, *The Books and the Parchments* (London: Pickerey & Ingles, 1950), pp. 94 ff. A more extensive treatment is by W. H. Green, *General Introduction to the Old Testament: the Canon* (London: Charles Scribner's, 1899), esp. pp. 9–156.

[2] Information about the education received by Jewish children in the time of Christ may be found in W. M. Ramsay, *The Education of Christ* (London: Hodder & Stoughton, 1902), pp. 61–67; Otho Fairfield Humphreys, *The Unknown Years of Jesus* (The Abba Company, 1924), pp. 77–87; and Alfred Edersheim, *The Life and Times of Jesus the Messiah*, I (New York: Longmans, Green, 1905), pp. 227–234.

Jesus heard the Scriptures read and expounded every Sabbath when He attended the synagogue service "as his custom was" (Luke 4:16). All that He learned became a storehouse of truth upon which He meditated "day and night" (Ps. 1:2).

Intuitively the Old Testament became His textbook of life.[3] His thought was literally cast in the spirit of the ancient patriarchs, kings, and prophets of Israel. Knowing their admonitions and experiences by heart, he used them "naturally and appositely."[4] So saturated was His utterance with the words and principles of Scripture, it is difficult to tell them apart. Where distinction can be made in the Gospels, there are at least ninety separate instances in which Jesus referred to the inspired Writings, either by direct quotation, allusion to an event, or language similar to biblical expressions.[5] Moreover, most of the Old Testament books are included in these refer-

---

[3] Probably the best all-round treatment of this subject is J. W. Wenham, *Christ and the Bible* (Downers Grove: InterVarsity Press, 1972), which is an update of his older *Our Lord's View of the Old Testament* (London: The Tyndale Press, 1953). Two published doctrinal dissertations also deserve notice: R. T. France, *Jesus and the Old Testament* (London: The Tyndale Press, 1971); and Robert P. Lightner, *The Saviour and the Scriptures* (Philadelphia: Presbyterian and Reformed Publishing Co., 1966). An older work, still useful, is by David James Burrell, *The Teaching of Jesus Concerning the Scriptures* (New York: American Tract Society, 1904). Excellent shorter studies are J. I. Packer, *Our Lord's Understanding of the Law of God* (1962); and R. V. G. Tasker, *Our Lord's Use of the Old Testament* (1953), both published by the Campbell Morgan Memorial Bible Lectureship, Westminster Chapel, Buckingham Gode, London, W.E. 1; also Jacob A. A. Preus, *It Is Written* (St. Louis: Concordia Publishing House, 1971); Clark H. Pinnock, *Biblical Revelation–The Foundation of Christian Theology* (Chicago: Moody Press, 1971) pp. 57–65; and his article, "The Inspiration of Scripture and the Authority of Jesus Christ," in *God's Inerrant Word*, ed. John W. Montgomery (Minneapolis: Bethany Fellowship, 1973), pp. 202–218.

[4] J. W. Wenham, *Christ and the Bible*, p. 29.

[5] Actually there are 160 references in the four Gospels where Jesus alludes to the Old Testament, counting duplication in parallel accounts. Approximately a hundred other references to the Jewish Scriptures are attributed to angels, prophets, Jesus' mother, the disciples, Pharisees and scribes, the people, or simply used in the narrative of events. Virtually a complete list of these references may be found in A. T. Robertson, *Harmony of the Gospels for Students of the Life of Christ* (New York: Harper & Brothers, 1922), pp. 295–301.

nces. This is even more impressive when one realizes that
He did not mention the extrabiblical literature of His day, nor
id He utilize the Apocryphal books.[6]

The Scriptures were for Jesus the light which revealed the
Father's will. They were in His mind as He prayed and fasted.
y them He withstood Satan's cunning attacks. They fur-
ished the substance of His teaching, whether counseling in
rivate or preaching to multitudes. In every kind of situation,
mid jubilation and in sorrow, with friend and with foe, when
ailed as a prophet and rejected as a blasphemer, the Holy
orah was the authority on which His life unfolded.

God's Written Word

Quite naturally Jesus spoke of the Scriptures as the "Word
f God" (John 10:35; Mark 7:13; cf. Luke 8:11, 12) or "the
ommandment of God" (Matt. 15:6). He knew they were in-
pired by the Holy Spirit, both in the concepts presented and
n the words used to communicate them. To Him, what the
criptures said, God said, and He often used the terms and
heir equivalents interchangeably (e.g., Matt. 19:4, 5; 21:16;
2:31; Mark 2:25; 12:10, 26; Luke 6:3).

Needless to say, with such a high view of inspiration, there
vas never any confusion in His thinking respecting the cred-
ability of the biblical witness.[7] In its whole and its parts the
Word as given by God is true. There is an awesome finality
bout it. When Jesus said, "It is written," the issue was set-
ed, for "the scripture cannot be broken" (John 10:35).[8] In His

---

[6] F. F. Bruce, *The Books and the Parchments*, p. 102.

[7] Narratives of the Old Testament are treated as factual history,
ncluding the persons and events mentioned, like the Genesis ac-
ount of man's creation (Matt. 19:4, 5; Mark 10:6–8); the blood of
Abel (Luke 11:51); Noah and the flood (Matt. 24:37–39; Luke 17:26,
7); Abraham (John 8:56); Lot and his wife (Luke 17:28–32); the
lestruction of Sodom (Matt. 10:15; 11:23, 24; Luke 10:12); the
preaching of Jonah, and the repentance of the Ninevites (Matt.
2:39–41; Luke 11:29–32), among others. For a full listing of refer-
nces, along with comment about the possibility of nonliteral in-
erpretation, see John W. Wenham, op. cit., pp. 12–16.

[8] This is even acknowledged by scholars of very liberal persuasion.
For example, D. Rudolf Bultman, most eminent of the radical critics,
ays that "Jesus agreed always with the scribes of his time in accept-
ng without question the authority of the (Old Testament) Law,"

view, "It is easier for heaven and earth to disappear than for
the least stroke of a pen to drop out of the Law" (Luke 16:17
NIV; cf. Matt. 5:18). A staggering assertion! For Christ, "a mere
tittle or jot of the written Word was of more value than all star
worlds and sun systems of the entire universe."[9]

Spiritually Perceived

But far more than mere mental acceptance is involved in
Jesus' view of Scripture. As the God-breathed Word, the divine oracles can be properly understood only in concurrence
with His Spirit.

An incident with the Sadducees, the scientific humanists of
the time, illustrates His position (Mark 12:18–27; Matt.
22:23–33; Luke 20:27–40).[10] These men asked Jesus about the
provision of the law whereby a widowed and childless woman

Jesus and the Word (New York: Charles Scribner's Sons, 1934), p. 61.
Likewise, F. C. Grant, well-known liberal author, commenting upon
the New Testament view of Scripture, notes: "Everywhere it is taken
for granted that what is written in scripture is the work of divine
inspiration, and is therefore trustworthy, infallible, and inerrant," *An
Introduction to New Testament Thought* (New York: Abingdon-
Cokesbury, 1950), p. 75. Another distinguished critic, H. J. Cadbury,
said that he was "far more sure as a mere historical fact that Jesus
held to the common Jewish view of an infallible Bible than that Jesus
believed in His own messiahship," quoted by Kenneth Kantzer,
"Christ and Scripture," *His*, January 1966, p. 17. By acknowledging
that Jesus held the prevailing view of Scripture in His day, of course,
liberal scholars do not mean to accept it themselves. But it does
create a problem for them. In seeking an explanation, some contend
that Christ's teaching about the Bible was merely an accommodation
to the popular feeling of the people, though this raises a serious
question about His honesty. Others believe that in becoming man,
Jesus assumed our limitations, even to the extent that He could make
mistakes in judgment. Such a position confuses the divine and
human natures in Christ, and, if followed through, makes His whole
teaching uncertain. For a good discussion of the results of question-
ing the inerrancy of Scripture, see Harold Lindsell, *The Battle for the
Bible* (Grand Rapids: Zondervan, 1976), esp. pp. 17–71, 141–160.
    [9] Erich Sauer, *The Dawn of World Redemption* (Grand Rapids:
Wm. B. Eerdmans, 1951), p. 11.
    [10] A refreshing treatment of this text, with a contemporary applica-
tion, is by John R. W. Stott in *Christ the Controversialist* (Downers
Grove: InterVarsity Press, 1970), pp. 49–64.

could be married to her deceased husband's brother, so that the dead man's family line might continue. The hypothetical question: Whose wife would she be in the resurrection if the woman had outlived seven husbands? Doubtless the Sadducees, who did not believe in an afterlife, thought they were terribly astute, and were going to make those supernaturalists look ridiculous.

Jesus' reply must have shocked them. "Ye do err," He said, "not knowing the scriptures, nor the power of God" (Matt. 22:29; cf. Mark 12:24). To explain, the Master referred to Moses' experience at the burning bush, where the Lord demonstrated that He was "not the God of the dead, but of the living" (Matt. 22:32; cf. Mark 12:27). God's purpose in creating man was that he might "live unto him" (Luke 20:38). For all their veneration of Moses, the Sadducees had missed the spiritual lesson of His teaching—not only in the continuation of life, but in the kind of experience one would have in the next world. Their thinking was so earthbound, it had not occurred to them that in the resurrection persons "neither marry, nor are given in marriage; but are as the angels which are in heaven" (Mark 12:25; cf. Matt. 22:30; Luke 20:35, 36).

In exposing their ignorance, Jesus made it plain that understanding the Scriptures requires a reverence in their presence. His answer to the question was to ask: "Have ye not read that which was spoken unto you by God?" (Matt. 22:31; cf. Mark 12:26). Obviously, whatever reading they had done was very superficial. Though professing to believe the Scripture, they did not know its Author. Hence, they were blind to the real power of God. That which is divinely inspired cannot be treated merely with academic interest. The Word demands obedience. Only in the responsive heart illumined by the Holy Spirit can one perceive His truth.

The Intent of Scripture

By pointing out the danger of unhallowed reason, Jesus showed how easy it is for a prejudiced mind to miss the deeper spiritual meaning of the Word. He was appalled, for example, that the Jews could be so concerned with the external minutiae of the Text, like tithing mint and anise and cummin, and leave undone the "weightier matters of the law, judgment, mercy, and faith" (Matt. 23:23; cf. Lev. 27:30; Mic. 6:8). That is why He was so indignant at the Pharisees, who sought to circumvent the intent of the Law through legalistic casuistry. Another case was their way of reneging on the duty to support aging parents by saying the money that could have been so used was already "corban," or devoted to God (Mark 7:10–13; Matt. 15:4–6; cf. Exod. 20:12; 21:17; Deut. 5:16; Lev. 20:9).

The problem centered in equating customary practice with Scripture. When the Pharisees condemned the apostolic company for disregarding tradition by eating with unwashed hands, Jesus responded: "You hypocrites! Isaiah was right when he prophesied about you: 'These people honor me with their lips, but their hearts are far from me. They worship me in vain; their teachings are but rules made by man' " (Matt. 15:7–9; Mark 7:6,7 NIV: cf. Isa. 29:13). However commendable their customs may have been, making them a matter of moral obligation nullified the Word of God (Matt. 15:6; Mark 7:13).

Jesus was simply asking that the original meaning of Scripture be respected in any interpretation. Human circumstances are always changing, but God's Word abides forever. In this context, He warned the Pharisees of their perversion of God's purpose for marriage by their cheap divorce proceedings (Matt. 19:1–12; Mark 10:1–12). Another time, when His hungry disciples were criticized for plucking corn on the Sabbath, He pointed out how God in the beginning had ordained the day for man's rest and blessing (Matt. 12:1–8; Mark 2:23–28; Luke 6:1–5). On the same basis, He answered those who objected to His healing on the Sabbath (Matt. 12:9–14; Mark 3:1–6; Luke 6:6–11). And when the scribes and Pharisees murmured because He ate with sinners, He alluded to the passage of Hosea, "I desire mercy, not sacrifice," He had told them: "But go and learn what this means" (Matt. 9:13 NIV). In each case, the implication was clear. Had the Jews understood the Scripture's intent, they would have been acting differently.

This was most obvious in the way they treated Jesus. Ostensibly they trusted the Law, but it was only a front. "If you believed Moses," Jesus reminded them, "you would believe me, for he wrote about me. But since you do not believe what he wrote, how are you going to believe what I say?" (John 5:46, 47 NIV). The common practice of the Jews was to read into the Scripture their own presuppositions and proud desires. Thus, their vision was obscured, and they missed its purpose: to "believe that Jesus is the Christ, the Son of God; and that believing [we] might have life through his name" (John 20:31).[11]

Fulfilled in Christ

Knowing that He was the fulfillment of the Old Testament prophecy, Jesus could tell the Jews to search the Scriptures, for "it is they that bear witness to me" (John 5:39 RSV). What a sense of awe and responsibility this knowledge must have given. For it meant that finally everything He did and said unfolded God's eternal Word. Nothing about His life was left to chance, or was incidental. He was the promised One, the Messiah who would bring deliverance to His people.

How Jesus came to understand this will always remain a mystery to us; but insofar as His human consciousness developed, the Scriptures must have been the decisive influence. It is significant that the only recorded incident about His childhood, when He was found in the Temple discussing questions with doctors of Law, indicates that the Law and the prophets absorbed His interest (Luke 2:46). When asked by Mary what He was doing, Jesus simply replied that He was about His "Father's business" (Luke 2:49).

The way He fit His ministry into the Old Testament portrait offers a fascinating study.[12] For example, He realized that His

---

[11] Again John Stott skillfully elaborates on this point in his discussion of "Scripture: End or Means?" *Christ the Controversialist*, op. cit. pp. 90–105.

[12] There are eleven references to Christ Himself explicitly calling attention to the fulfillment of Scripture, along with a few statements alluding to the future fulfillment of Bible prophecies (e.g., Luke 21:24, 32; 22:16; Mark 13:30; Matt. 24:34). In addition, the Gospel writers make mention of the definite fulfillment of Scripture more than twenty times. For example, Matthew notes that Jesus settles in Capernaum, in the borders of Zebulun and Naphtali as the prophet had said (Matt. 4:13–16; cf. Isa. 9:1, 2). Actually, we can see the Old

association with John the Baptist was an answer to the prophecy regarding the coming of Elijah (Matt. 11:7–15, 17:11, 12; Luke 7:24–28; Mark 9:12, 13; cf. Mal. 3:1; 4:5). Imbued with a scriptural zeal for keeping God's house pure, His first act upon going to Jerusalem was to cleanse the Temple of the corrupting money changers (John 2:15–17; cf. Ps. 69:9); an act repeated at the end of His ministry (Mark 11:15–17; Matt. 21:12, 13; Luke 19:45, 46; cf. Isa. 56:7; Jer.7:11). With the same sense of direction, He preached to the poor, healed the sick, opened the eyes of the blind, and cast out demons, to fulfill that which had been spoken by the prophet (Luke 4:17–21; 7:18–23; Matt. 8:16, 17; 11:2–6; 12:5–21; Mark 9:9–13; cf. Isa. 29:18, 19; 35:5, 6; 58:6; 61:1, 2). There is always the assurance that He was only doing what the Bible said He would do.

That His ministry would be rejected by the Jews came as no surprise, for as He pointed out, it was written: "This people's heart is waxed gross, and their ears are dull of hearing, and their eyes they have closed; lest at any time they should see with their eyes, and hear with their ears, and should understand with their heart, and should be converted, and I should heal them" (Matt. 13:14, 15; cf. Isa. 6:6–10). Calling attention to Micah's prophecy, He confided to His disciples that He had come "to set a man at variance against his father, and the daughter against her mother . . . . And a man's foes shall be they of his own household" (Matt. 10:35, 36; cf. Mic. 7:6). Yet, if it was any consolation, His knowledge of the Old Testament assured Him that "a prophet is not without honour, save in his own country" (Matt. 13:57; cf. Mark 6:4).

Testament's portrait of Christ, in typology, teaching, and prophecy, implicitly unfolding all through the Gospels. To open the wider dimensions of this theme, the student will want to consult some of the studies which deal with it in depth, such as Wilhelm Vischer's two-volume, *The Witness of the Old Testament to Christ*, trans. A. B. Crabtree (London: Lutterworth Press, 1949); Alfred Edersheim, *Prophecy and History in Relation to the Messiah* (New York: Anson D. F. Randolf, 1885); Charles Augustus Briggs, *Messianic Prophecy* (New York: Charles Scribner's, 1889); Patrick Fairbairn, *The Typology of Scripture*, reprinted (Grand Rapids: Zondervan, n.d.); and, above all, E. W. Hengstenberg's monumental four-volume work, *Christology of the Old Testament and a Commentary on the Messianic Predictions* (Grand Rapids: Kregel, 1956, © 1872–78).

When the time of His passion drew near, remembering how Zechariah had said that the King would come into Jerusalem riding upon a donkey, He obtained such an animal on which to make His entry into the city (Matt. 21:1-9; Mark 11:1-7; John 12:13, 14; cf. Zech. 9:9; Isa. 63:11). The people's compulsive, though superficial, shouts of "Hosanna" in the streets and in the Temple, could be understood in the light of the Psalmist's prophecy (Matt. 21:9, 16; Mark 11:9, 10; Luke 19:38; cf. Ps. 8:2; 118:24, 26). He realized that those He had befriended would turn against Him, that the Word might be fulfilled: "They hated me without a cause" (John 15:25; cf. Ps. 35:19; 69:4). Even His own disciples would falter, and finally run away, for the prophet had said: "I will smite the shepherd, and the sheep of the flock shall be scattered" (Matt. 26:31; Mark 14:27; cf. Zech. 13:7). Most tragically one of them, according to the Scriptures, would betray Him for thirty pieces of silver (Mark 14:21; Matt. 26:46; John 13:18; 17:12; cf. Ps. 41:9; Zech. 11:12).

Suffering and Death

In His scripturally conditioned mind, Jesus knew all along that He would be made a spectacle before the sin-cursed world, like Moses lifted up the serpent in the wilderness (John 3:14; cf. Num. 21:8, 9). What had been alluded to many times with the disciples was expressed graphically at His last Passover supper, when He broke the bread as a symbol of His broken body; then poured out the red wine, and said: "This is my blood of the new testament, which is shed for many" (Mark 14:24; Matt. 26:28; Luke 22:20; 1 Cor. 11:25; cf. Exod. 24:8; Lev. 4:18-20; Jer. 31:31-33; Zech. 9:11; Isa. 53:11). In these words He summed up the essence of all the Old Testament offerings.[13] Knowing the meaning of the Scripture, of course, did not diminish the agony of His ordeal, as in the Garden where He drank the cup of God's fury against man's sin, but it did assure Him that it was to be expected (Mark 14:34; Matt. 26:38; cf. Ps. 42:6; Isa. 51:22). When the Temple crowd came out with swords and staves to seize Him, God's Word was His stay (Mark 14:49; Matt. 26:56). He could have

---

[13] A thorough study of this concept, along with bibliographic sources, may be found in my book *Written in Blood*.

escaped the humiliation that awaited Him by summoning twelve legions of angels to His rescue. But He answered this suggestion: "How then shall the scriptures be fulfilled, that thus it must be?" (Matt. 26:54).

So it was that He suffered in patience when condemned by sinners (Matt. 26:60–63; cf. Ps. 27:12; 35:11; Isa. 53:7); when smitten and spat upon (Mark 14:65; 15:17; Matt. 26:67; John 19:1–3; cf. Isa. 50:6); and, finally, when crucified between two thieves (Matt. 27:38; Mark 15:27, 28; Luke 23:33; cf. Isa. 53:12). Moreover, the Scriptures foretold the mockery heaped upon Him as He died (Matt. 27:39–44; Mark 15:29–32; cf. Ps. 22:6–8). In His anguish, He recalled the ancient prophecies and prayed for His antagonizers (Luke 23:34; cf. Isa. 53:12), while soldiers cast lots for His garments (Mark 15:24; Matt. 27:35; John 19:23, 24; cf. Ps. 22:18). Feeling totally abandoned, He cried to God in words imprinted on His mind from the Psalms (Matt. 27:46; Mark 15:34; cf. Ps. 22:1). Remembering one more prophecy, Jesus groaned in thirst, whereupon there was pushed to His lips a sponge filled with vinegar (Matt. 27:48, 49; Mark 15: 36; John 19:28, 29; cf. Ps. 69:21). Then having fulfilled every detail previously specified by the Spirit (John 19:30), He offered up His life to the Father, dying with words of Scripture on His lips (Luke 23:46; cf. Ps. 31:5).

By the same biblical criteria, Christ knew that the Son of Man would rise again in glory and be seated at the right hand of God.[14] It was all spelled out in the Book. There were no coincidences or mistakes. From beginning to end, His life was the fulfillment of "all that the prophets have spoken" (Luke 24:25). As He said to the two disciples going to Emmaus on the day of His Resurrection: "Ought not Christ to have suffered these things, and to enter into his glory?" Then "beginning at Moses and all the prophets, he expounded unto them in all the scriptures the things concerning himself" (Luke 24:26, 27).

Fulfilling the Law

This same sense of fulfillment of Scripture comes through in Jesus' teaching, of which the Sermon on the Mount is a good

---

[14] Prophecies relating to His future reign will be discussed in chapter 6.

example.[15] Before laying down the ethical principles in the message, Jesus explained: "Think not that I am come to destroy the law, or the prophets: I am not come to destroy, but to fulfil" (Matt. 5:17). He did not want anyone to think that His teaching superseded the old Revelation. Quite the contrary, He believed that "one jot or one tittle shall in no wise pass from the law, till all be fulfilled" (Matt. 5:18; cf. Luke 16:17). A solemn warning was left with anyone who broke even one of the least commandments (Matt. 5:19).

In His insistence upon the infallibility of Scripture, however, Jesus carefully pointed out the difference between popular interpretations and the God-given message (Matt. 5:21–48). He referred to such false assumptions as loving your neighbor implies hating your enemy; or murder and adultery pertain only to specific acts, and not attitudes; or one has to keep his word only when a certain kind of oath is made. To refute these errors Jesus presented the correct meaning in His own words. In so doing, He did not subordinate the old Law; rather, He exposed its essence in life application.

What He did was to locate the biblical mandate in the nature of God. He was not interested in imposing upon man a lot of austere regulations to create an appearance of religiosity. God made man in His own image, and consistent with this nature, He wants man to be perfected in His love (Matt. 5:48), a love for God that finds expression in loving our neighbor as we love ourselves (Matt. 22:36–40; Luke 6:31; cf. Deut. 6:4, 5; 10:19; Lev. 19:18). The story of the good Samaritan is an illustration of the law in practice (Luke 10:30–37). Jesus taught that the Scripture is fulfilled, not by reciting orthodox creeds, nor by going through religious rites, but by loving as we have

---

[15] There are a number of special treatments of the Sermon on the Mount available for further study. W. D. Davies, *The Setting of the Sermon on the Mount* (Cambridge: At the University Press, 1964) gives a good historical approach. For exposition of the text, among the best are D. Martyn Lloyd-Jones' two-volume, *Studies in the Sermon on the Mount* (London: InterVarsity, 1959–60); Arthur W. Pink, *An Exposition of the Sermon on the Mount* (Grand Rapids: Baker, 1958); and Hans Ludwig Wendisch, *The Meaning of the Sermon on the Mount*, trans. S. MacLean Gilmour (Philadelphia: Westminster, 1951). Various interpretations are explained by Harvey K. McArthur in *Understanding the Sermon on the Mount* (New York: Harper, 1960).

been loved. Such love cannot be self-contained, but will issue in acts of ministry, particularly to persons in obvious need—giving freely to the oppressed; forgiving those through whom we have suffered wrong; blessing those who have cursed us; doing good to them that hate us. This is the way God has acted toward us, and as He has shown mercy, so we are to be merciful (Luke 6:36; Matt. 7:11). The Father expects only our gratitude for His love toward us by our doing joyfully what He wills (Matt. 7:21).

The summons is to true discipleship—faithfully living by the Word of God. Jesus' own obedience becomes the perfect example. As the Father loved Him, so He has loved us (John 15:9, 10). His great commandment is simply that we love the same way (John 15:12, 17).[16] When all is said and done, such a life sums up everything that is written in the Law and the prophets (Matt. 7:12).

The Word of Christ

By such teaching, Jesus claimed for Himself the same authority invested in Scripture, and that thereafter, people would be accountable for what they did with His testimony. "Therefore, everyone who hears these words of mine and puts them into practice" would endure, He said, whereas "everyone who hears these words of mine and does not put them into practice" would perish (Matt. 7:24–27 NIV). He made these assertions on the basis of His inherent relationship with God. This authority was especially pronounced when He declared, "I say unto you," or the more emphatic form, "Verily, verily, I say unto you." [17] He knew His message

---

[16] A new aspect of this commandment, not specifically stated before, is that we are to love "just as" ($\kappa\alpha\theta\grave{\omega}\varsigma$) Jesus has loved us. This may have been implied under the old Law, but now it is enunciated explicitly. The same transference relates also to the communion one sustains with Christ (e.g., John 6:57; 15:4; 17:11) and His mission (e.g. John 17:18; 20:21). Only when this expectation sinks in can we begin to fathom the necessity and provision of God's grace.

[17] The words *verily, verily,* or literally, *amen, amen,* are Hebrew terms coming through Aramaic which mean "certainly." Used about sixty times in the Gospels preceding Jesus' words "I say unto you" ($\lambda\acute{\epsilon}\gamma\omega\ \acute{\nu}\mu\iota\nu$), the expression accents the complete validity of the

was not given in isolation: "I have not spoken of myself; but the Father which sent me, he gave me a commandment, what I should say, and what I should speak. And I know that his commandment is life everlasting: whatsoever I speak therefore, even as the Father said unto me, so I speak" (John 12:49, 50; cf. 3:34; 7:16, 17; 14:10, 24; 17:8, 14).

Borne along with this sense of divine authenticity, He never hesitated with doubt, nor apologized for errors in judgment. Yet from the confines of His human nature, He frankly acknowledged His limitations of knowledge (e.g., Mark 13:32; Matt. 24:36), an honesty which only enhances our appreciation of His integrity. He knew what He did not know as a man, and His pointing out this fact makes us more certain that what He did speak was the truth. Never did Jesus offer an opinion subject to rebuttal, nor even venture an hypothesis relatively correct, for He realized that every word He spoke would count for eternity. Ultimately those who repeat what He said will be judged by those same words "in the last day" (John 12:48).

Indeed, in this consciousness, Jesus identified His speech with the life-giving power of His Spirit: "The words that I speak unto you, they are spirit, and they are life" (John 6:63). There is no distinction between what He taught and how He communicated the message. His words are declared synonymous with the Spirit of truth: "I tell you the truth, whoever hears my word and believes him who sent me has eternal life" (John 5:24 NIV: cf. 8:51). By the same token, obedience to His Word is the instrument through which disciples are made (John 8:31, 32); the heart cleansed (John 15:3; cf. 17:17); divine fellowship established (John 14:15, 16, 23; 17:6); and prayer answered (John 15:7).

Clearly the Spirit which controlled His life was seen in His

---

statement, and carries the weight of divine authority. It is remarkably similar to the Old Testament formula "Thus saith the Lord," used about 3500 times by the prophets to show that their message comes from God, not their own wisdom. An excellent discussion of this concept is by Joachim Jeremias, *New Testament Theology*, pp. 35–36, 251–255. In connection with *Amen*, Kittel's *Theological Dictionary of the New Testament* I adds a pertinent comment: "The one who accepts His word as true and certain is also the one who acknowledges and affirms it in his own life, and thus causes it, as fulfilled by him, to become a demand to others," p. 338.

daily speech. This, coupled with His mighty works, compelled attention. The people could see that His "word was with power" (Luke 4:32; cf. 4:36). "He taught them as one having authority, and not as the scribes" (Matt. 7:29; cf. Mark 1:22–28). Even the officers who plotted to kill Him admitted in consternation, "Never man spake like this man" (John 7:46). But those most impressed by His words were the disciples, who, recognizing that He lived as He spoke, resolutely affirmed that He had come from God (John 16:30).

Delegated Authority

It was to these chosen men who knew Him best that He entrusted His apostleship (Luke 6:12, 13; Mark 3:14).[18] Appointing them to be with Him, for three years He taught them the mysteries of the Kingdom of God (Mark 4:11). The words which He received from the Father were given unto them (John 17:8, 14). They in turn were expected to pass the message on to others (John 17:20). As we have seen, His promised charisma of the Holy Spirit relates to this transmission process. Thus, that One who had inspired the Scriptures, and who had spoken through the Son, was to take His Word and defuse it through the apostles to the ends of the earth.

With this authority they went forth as emissaries of Christ. Their words and deeds attest to their confidence in Him who sent them (e.g., Acts 2:14–40; 3:6, 7; 10:41, 42; 1 Thess. 2:13). Moreover, the Church honored their witness, preserving a continuity of doctrine with the apostles, while also making possible stability and order in their fellowship.

In time the oral teachings of the apostles were committed to writing under the Spirit's guidance (2 Tim. 3:16; 2 Pet. 1:20, 21; 1 Cor. 2:13). Those who were inspired to write the New Testament did not add to Christ's words, but interpreted and applied them in a new setting. These documents conveyed

---

[18] The word *apostle* (ὑπόστολος) means "sent one," the emphasis being upon definite purpose and authority as on a mission. J. Norvel Geldenhuys notes in his study of this concept, *Supreme Authority*, that the term as used in the New Testament takes on the meaning of "one chosen and sent with a special commission as the fully authorized representative of the sender" (Grand Rapids: Wm. B. Eerdmans, 1953), pp. 53, 54. See also note 1 Chapter 5.

the authority of Jesus Himself, and were so recognized by the Church.[19] Attesting to their authority, passages from these books were read in early Christian worship services along with the Old Testament Scriptures. Thus the Scripture became the sole rule for faith and practice.

In the ensuing years these inspired words were entrusted to faithful men, who also taught them to others (2 Tim. 2:2), until finally the message comes to us. Believing the message brings one into the apostolic succession of our Lord's doctrine and mission. The process cannot end in this world until all have heard. Just as Jesus taught His disciples, so we must teach ours, and send them forth with His authority.[20]

Mastered by the Word

This places a high priority upon learning the Word of God. Jesus has given us the example. As the incarnate Word, of course, He did not have to refer to the Scriptures to show His authority. In His divine wisdom He could have expressed His mind, as He often did, without recourse to what God had said before. But the fact that He still chose to bind His words by the Scriptures underscores the Bible's importance. If in the plan of God it was deemed necessary for God's Son to measure His life by Holy Writ, surely our need is no less real.

Of this we can be sure: The only enduring worth of our witness is that verified in the Word. Nothing else we say or do has any real significance to the Gospel. God disclosed Himself in words—words spoken by His prophets, written in the Scrip-

---

[19] The New Testament books began to be written about A.D. 45, and their production continued until the end of the century. Collections of these writings appear in the second century, though it was still later before those bearing the marks of divine inspiration were gathered into the canon of the Church. See F. F. Bruce, *The Books and the Parchments*, pp. 102–111; and Donald Guthrie, *New Testament Introduction*, p. 566 ff.

[20] There is an important difference between authority, which rests on revealed truth, and being authoritarian, which comes out of dogmatism. The latter restricts whereas the former liberates. By the same criterion, Christians should have a tolerant attitude toward those who disagree, loving them, regardless of differences, while maintaining an unnegotiable attitude toward the truth of the Gospel (Eph. 4:15; Gal. 1:6–9; 1 Cor. 13:7).

tures, and finally, personified in His Son. All that had been
said before Christ's coming was significant in anticipation of
Him; all that has been inspired since His coming has significance by virtue of its fulfillment in Him. His life is wedded
to His Word, so much so that His Words given unto the disciples are the means by which the world will come to know
Him. Evangelism, in this sense, is making known words—
words disclosing Christ, and His redeeming grace.

Through the Word, our lives, too, are conformed to Him
who is the object of all that is written. Thus, it is the Word
believed that regenerates the heart (1 Pet. 1:23; 2 Pet. 1:4),
and sets us apart as His possession (John 17:17, 19; Eph. 5:26).
This is the food upon which our spirits feed (1 Pet. 2:2),
whereby we are built up in faith, and given an inheritance
among the sanctified (Acts 20:32). By the same testimony we
have joy, and peace, and security forevermore (Ps. 119; 1 John
1:4; Acts 15:31; Rom. 15:14). Truly it is the Word of Life (Phil.
2:16): the more we live in its truth, the more we will become
like Him who is the living Word of God, and will want to share
His life with others.

4

His Understanding of the Gospel

As the Word of God, Jesus spoke to the real need of the world. He knew the sinfulness of man, and its dreadful consequence. He also knew how man could be redeemed by the grace of God, and His ministry was predicated upon this knowledge.

The High Estate of Man

Christ never lost sight of the purpose of man. He knew that man was created for the glory of God, to enjoy His fellowship in loving obedience, and to worship and serve Him forever (Matt. 4:10; 5:16; cf. Deut. 6:13). Only within this relationship to God can man experience true dignity and fulfillment.

Nothing is more tragic than for the creature to ignore this fact and seek first the fleshly pleasures of this world. As Jesus explained, a man's worth is not to be measured by the abundance of material "things" (Luke 12:15). Man is made to be a spiritual personality, and as such can only live by the Word "that proceedeth out of the mouth of God" (Matt. 4:4). Sheer sanity should cause him to recognize that he is totally dependent upon the sustaining care of his Maker. Still, as a moral being, he is free to choose which way to go—whether to serve God or mammon (Matt. 6:24; Luke 16:13; cf. vss. 9, 11).[1] The

---

[1] *Mammon* is a word which occurs these four times on the lips of Jesus in the New Testament. It refers to earthly goods or property, always in the derogatory sense of being antigodly. This materialistic outlook characterizes natural man who lays up treasures upon earth

Father will not violate man's integrity, but He makes the choice clear, and by every persuasion under heaven, He seeks to woo him to the highest good.

Jesus demonstrated this higher life, thus showing God's purpose for every man. His consuming passion was to glorify the Father who sent Him (John 13:31; 14:13; 17:1, 4, 5). In this hallowed obedience, He experienced an infinite sense of divine fellowship and perfect peace. Before returning to heaven, He asked Mary to tell His disciples: "I ascend unto my Father, and your Father; and to my God, and your God" (John 20:17), indicating the continuity of His life with all those who believe on Him. As everyone participated in His suffering, so all have the privilege of sharing His glory. Man's ultimate value can only be measured by the destiny of the victorious Son of Man.

Guided by this criterion of value, Jesus knew the worth of a soul. Outward appearances were to Him but a momentary circumstance. The real self was His concern. He could see the true person whether clad in beggar's rags or prince's robes. The immortal soul, however defaced by neglect, was made for a higher destiny than any other created being—to reign with Christ in the Kingdom of His holiness in an ever-expanding experience of God's eternal love.[2] How could such unspeakable satisfaction be compared to the fleeting pleasures of this world? Though a man had every indulgence of the flesh satisfied, what would he gain in the end if he forfeited "his true self" (Matt. 16:26 NEB)?

(cf. Matt. 6:19–34; Luke 12:15–34). Seeking first the things of this world, man becomes enslaved to them, for what one devotes himself to becomes his god (Matt. 6:21). See Kittel, IV, op. cit., pp. 289, 390. This craving of man for "mammon," as an attitude of worldlings, may be seen in various ways throughout the ministry of Jesus. For example, it is apparent in the desire of the multitudes to make Jesus king so that He might satisfy their physical desires (John 6:15; Luke 19:11–17); or the repeated request that Jesus show signs of His power (Mark 8:12; Matt. 16:4; John 12:37). Perhaps its most vivid demonstration comes out in Judas (John 12:4–6).

[2] The concept of the Kingdom, a truth entwined in the Gospel, will be discussed in connection with the vision of Christ in chapter 6.

The Human Tragedy

Yet this was the condition that Jesus saw every time He looked out upon the multitude. Inflated with egotism, the creature had forsaken his true glory and turned to his own way. Like the prodigal son, he had left his father's house, and gone into a far country where he squandered his inheritance in riotous living. Now deprived of his once high estate, man was destitute, famished in spirit, living like the swine in the mire (Luke 15:11–16).

This picture of willful failure to live as God intended underlies Jesus' description of the human tragedy. Sin is coming short of God's expectations, whether the deviation occurs by omission or commission.[3] The creature is under judgment be-

---

[3] Jesus does not develop a theological definition for sin, but rather deals with the fact of its presence. What He means by it can be deduced from the various words used in His teaching. The most common term, ἀμαρτία, used more than fifty times in its various cognate forms, conveys the idea of missing the mark, as when a man throws a spear and does not strike the target. In this case the mark is God's character and Law which has been missed (e.g., Matt. 9:2, 5, 6; 18:15; Luke 15:18, 21; 17:3, 4; John 5:14; 8:11, 24, 34, 9:34, 41). The word implies a moral responsibility for the sin, whether conscious or not. It may reflect the aggregate of sins committed, either by an individual or a group. The word *sinner* belongs to this same family. Other important terms, used less often by Jesus, are: ἀδικία ("unrighteousness" or "injustice"), stressing conduct incongruous with God's nature (e.g., Luke 13:27; 16:8; 18:6; John 7:18); ἀνομία (usually translated "iniquity" or "lawlessness"), describing the condition of one without law, either by ignorance or transgression (Matt. 7:23; 13:41; 23:28; 24:12); and παράπτωμα (denoting "trespassing" or "misdeeds" deliberate or unintentional—e.g. Matt. 6:14, 15; 18:35). The word *evil* or *wicked* (πονηρός) also should be noted. It is used by Jesus about forty times in the Gospels with reference to that which is bad in human nature (e.g., Matt. 7:11, 17, 18; 9:4; 12:34, 35; 15:19; Mark 7:22, 23), as well as the demonic world (e.g., Matt. 12:45; 13:19, 38; Luke 7:21; 8:2; 11:26; John 17:15). There is in the word an overtone of calamity, particularly its cause. Much the same thrust comes out in ψαθλος, also translated "evil," in John 3:20 and 5:29; and κακία, used only in Matt. 6:34 in the Gospels. A brief discussion of these terms may be found in G. Campbell Morgan, *The Teaching of Christ*, pp. 130–134. For the Greek description, any good lexicon will suffice, such as William F. Arndt and F. Wilbur Gingrich, *A Greek-English Lexicon of the New Testament* (Chicago: University of

cause he has perverted what he was meant to be, like salt which has lost its savor (Matt. 5:13), or a tree which does not yield good fruit (Matt. 7:18, 19; cf. Luke 13:6–9). The Lord of creation expects man to develop his potential as a wise steward of His trust (Matt. 24:14–30; cf. 19:13–29). Not to do so displays a spirit of unbelief, and is an affront to heaven.

Failing to seek his own good, man also has no sensitivity to his neighbor's need. He acts like the priest and the Levite who passed by the wounded Samaritan (Luke 10:30–37) or the rich Dives who closed his ears to the beggar's cry at the city gate (Luke 16:19–31; cf. Matt. 18:21–35). Of course, by scorning a fellow human being he is actually sinning against Christ. "Whatever you did not do for one of the least of these," Jesus said, "you did not do for me" (Matt. 25:45 NIV).

Ultimately all sin strikes at the character of God. It is not so much the breaking of His law, as it is the scorning of His love. Man will not accept the Father's will. Whether expressed through unconscious apathy or overt acts of defiance, the creature, crazed by conceit, flaunts his own sovereignty and enthrones himself as the master of his destiny. Self-centeredness dominates life in every direction.

Deceitfulness of the Heart

Making the rebellion more pathetic, man likes to hide his pride under the adornment of goodness, especially in the guise of religion. This was developed into a fine art by the Pharisees. They meticulously kept the external demands of the law—tithing all their produce (Matt. 23:23), giving alms to the poor, observing set hours for prayer, fasting twice a week (Matt. 6:1–18), compassing land and sea to make one proselyte (Matt. 23:15)—but their motive was wrong. They went through th exercises of piety to be recognized and acclaimed for their own righteousness (Matt. 23:5). God's love was not in it. Jesus did not condemn them for their zeal, but for their

---

Chicago Press, 1957), pp. 17, 18, 42, 43, 71, 624, 697; and Joseph Henry Thayer, *A Greek-English Lexicon of the New Testament* (New York: American Book Co., 1886), pp. 12, 30, 31, 48, 49, 320, 485, 530, 650. Also, the serious student will want to survey the information in Kittel, op. cit., especially I, pp. 149–163; 267–316; and IV, pp. 546–566.

hypocrisy—pretending to be something they were not.[4] So complete was their deception that they considered everyone but themselves sinners (Matt. 9:11; 11:19; Mark 2:16; Luke 5:30; 15:1; 19:7; John 9:16, 24).

The irony is that the moralistic Jews failed to take sin seriously. Though careful to avoid certain obvious forms of wickedness, like murder and adultery, they ignored the underlying hatred and lust which found expression in more subdued, but no less real, forms of perversion (Matt. 5:21, 22, 25). In their preoccupation with performance, even gradating what sins were of less consequence than others, they simply did not reckon with the inner corruption of human nature.[5] Jesus made it clear that mere conformity to rules and regulations did not get to the basic problem. "For from within, out of men's hearts, come evil thoughts, sexual immorality, theft, murder, adultery, greed, malice, deceit, lewdness, envy, slander, arrogance and folly. All these evils come from inside and make a man 'unclean' " (Mark 7:21–23 NIV; cf. Matt. 15:19, 20). Until those who kept the externals of the Law also reckoned with their inner perverseness, they were blind to reality (John 8:44; 9:39–41). Nor could their witness lead others into the Kingdom (Matt. 23:3). An evil tree cannot bring forth good fruit (Matt. 7:16–20).

No wonder the Pharisees were offended by this teaching! Everything they had worked so hard to achieve was seen by Jesus as a display of vanity. Even their philanthropic generosity in building memorials to venerate the prophets was a cover-up for their iniquity (Matt. 23:29–32). They were like those very whitewashed tombs, glistening with beauty on the

---

[4] The word for *hypocrite* (ὑποκριτής) means playactor. It denotes one who plays a role as if on a stage. In its religious setting, then, a hypocrite is one who acts out a lie. Such persons, next to His betrayer, receive Jesus' strongest condemnation (Matt. 6:2, 5, 16; 7:5; 15:7; 16:3; 22:18; 23:13–29; 24:51; Mark 7:6; Luke 6:42; 11:44; 12:56; 13:15).

[5] The Jewish Torah lists 248 commandments and 365 prohibitions, the breaking of which constitutes sin. Within this catalogue, distinctions are made between greater and lesser sins, conscious and unconscious. An insightful treatment of this misguided practice, and its consequence, under the heading "The piety that separates from God," may be found in Joachim Jeremias, *New Testament Theology*, pp. 147–151.

outside but full of putrefaction within (Matt. 23:27, 28). Their
hearts were filled with extortion and self-indulgence (Matt.
23:25). With shocking bluntness, Jesus called them "blind
guides" (Matt. 23:16, 24), "serpents," "a generation of vipers"
(Matt. 12:34; 23:33). Though having the appearance of sheep,
they actually had the character of "ravening wolves" (Matt.
7:15).

Universal Depravity

Those who loved the uppermost seats in the synagogues
were not alone in their depravity. While they may have been
under greater condemnation for their hypocrisy, the whole
human race shared the same twisted sense of moral integrity.
It was a generation described as "evil," "wicked," "sinful,"
and "faithless" (Matt. 7:11; 12:38–45; 16:4; Mark 8:38, 9:19;
Luke 11:29). In their degeneracy, they were like that people
in Noah's day, eating, drinking, taking wives and husbands as
they pleased (Matt. 24:37–39; cf. Luke 17:26–29). Jesus compared them to children sitting in the market place, gleefully
fiddling away their opportunities for redemption (Matt.
11:16–19; Luke 7:31–35; cf. 21:35). Despite their cunning
(Luke 16:8), they had no perception of spiritual truth (John
14:17; 17:25). Individually and collectively, they were all
"workers of iniquity" (Luke 13:27).

In consequence, haughty, boastful, presumptuous man was
a "servant of sin" (John 8:34). He was lost in the labyrinth of
the world (Matt. 10:6; 15:24; 18:11; 21:41; Luke 15:4, 6, 8, 9,
24, 32; 19:10).[6] There was no way in his own ingenuity that he
could find his way to God. In terms of spiritual vitality, apart

---

[6] The word *lost* ($\alpha\pi\acute{o}\lambda\lambda\upsilon\mu\iota$), going back to the Hebrew, is the fault
of the one who suffers it. It can also mean perish or destroy, which is
the connotation most often seen in the seventy instances in which the
word occurs in the Gospels, for example, Matt. 2:13; 5:29, 30; 9:17;
10:28; 12:14; 22:7; 26:52; Mark 1:24; 3:6; 9:22; 11:18; 12:9; Luke
4:34; 5:37; 8:24; 9:56; 11:51; 13:3, 5, 33; 15:17; 17:27, 29; 19:47;
21:18; John 3:15, 16; 6:27; 10:10, 28; 11:50. The word is linked to
$\dot{\alpha}\pi\acute{\omega}\lambda\epsilon\iota\alpha$, meaning "ruin" or "destruction," not extinction of existence, but a state of everlasting torment (e.g., Matt. 7:13). See Kittel,
I, op. cit., p. 377.

from divine intervention, mankind was already "dead" (Luke 9:60; 15:32; cf. John 8:21, 24).

The rejection of the One sent from God to bear witness to the Light was proof of man's utter depravity (John 1:8, 9). They could not even recognize the face of God's Son when He appeared among them. "He was in the world, and the world was made by him, and the world knew him not. He came unto his own, and his own received him not" (John 1:10, 11). Blaspheming the Holy Spirit and showing their contempt for truth, they rejected Christ, whose every act and word was one of love. This was their condemnation: that light had come into the world, and they "loved darkness rather than light, because their deeds were evil" (John 3:19). Like the guests bidden to the great feast, they were too occupied with their own self-indulgence to heed the gracious invitation of the king (Matt. 22:1–10; Luke 14:16–24).

Satanic Deception

In choosing mammon against God, the sinful creature manifests his allegiance to another master. "You belong to your father, the devil, and you want to carry out your father's desire," stated Jesus (John 8:44 NIV; cf. 8:23). This is strong teaching. It is not that men are descendants of Beelzebub, but that they are under Satanic influence, and unwittingly participate in his evil design to subvert the work of God.

Jesus gave no specific explanation of the origin of the demonic conspiracy, but He was under no illusion about its existence and extent. Satan was recognized as a personal adversary (Matt. 4:10; 10:25; 12:26, 27; 25:41; Mark 3:22; 4:15, Luke 8:12); the embodiment of all that is evil (Matt. 13:19, 38, 39); a murderer and liar from the beginning (John 8:44); the aspirant ruler of this world (John 12:31; 14:30; 16:11). As the enemy of God and man, he directs a vast network of incorporeal spiritual beings endued with superhuman strength and intelligence defused through every strata of society. No one could be more naive than to be unmindful of this insidious power.[7]

---

[7] Regrettably, there are some who contend that Jesus was either mistaken in His belief or merely going along with the prevalent be-

Jesus knew that this domain of Satan is militantly arrayed
against the Kingdom of righteousness. The devil is ever seeking to tempt and mislead (Matt. 4:10; 6:13), trying to take away
God's Word from the heart of man (Matt. 13:19, 37–39; Mark
4:15; Luke 8:12), and to pull down the faithful (Matt. 16:23;
Luke 22:31). Not content merely with deception, unclean
spirits can captivate one's personality, bringing torment to the
mind and affliction to the body.[8] Their mission is to destroy
that which is good: it is always negative, the spirit of Anti-
christ. Whether taking the form of violent disruption, as with
the Gadarene demoniacs, or in the guise of moral refinement,
as with the self-righteous Pharisees, the end result is the
same. Man in his rebellious state is in subjection to "the evil
one."

---

liefs of His time. Those who follow this reasoning usually interpret
references to demons as some kind of mental disorder. A more
sophisticated denial of the reality is to look upon all human personality as possessing a demonic ingredient, thus resolving the problem in
a sort of psychological war between God and Satan.

[8] Demoniacs, persons overcome by evil spirits, are mentioned
many times in the Gospels. General references are in Mark 1:34, 39;
3:11, where the casting out of demons is linked to Jesus' ministry of
healing, teaching and preaching. Specific accounts may be found in
Matt. 8:28–34; 9:27–34; 12:22–37; 15:21–28; 17:14–20; Mark 1:21–28;
3:19–30; 5:1–20; 7:24–30; 9:14–29; Luke 4:34–39; 8:22, 26–39; 9:37–
43. Only in the case of Judas is the devil personally involved (John
13:27). How a demon can enter the body of a person is not disclosed,
but it would seem the result of weakness in the face of attack. One
evil spirit may bring in others, spirits even more wicked, so that the
individual's condition may become worse (Luke 11:24–26). Sometimes they gain such control that the victim loses his own personality.
It is evident, too, that demons can cause mental and physical anguish.
However, the Gospel writers carefully distinguish between demon-
caused diseases and those which are not (e.g., Matt. 4:23, 24; 8:16, 17;
Mark 1:34; Luke 4:40, 41). Significantly, demons know that they are
defeated by Christ, whom they recognize as the Son of God, the Lord
of heaven and earth (Matt. 8:31, 32; Mark 1:24). That is why they
obey His command, though often not without a struggle. In every
case where Jesus confronts demons in the Gospels, they are defeated.
He has no fear of them. Nor should those who believe in His name.
Demons must yield to the Word of God (Mark 3:14, 15; 6:7, 16:17;
Matt. 10:1; Luke 9:1; 10:1; cf. Acts 16:18; 19:15).

Eternal Death

The servitude of man to evil must have been grievous for the Master to bear, but the knowledge of its ultimate result caused Him even greater suffering. He realized that the penal issues of sin remain unchanged unless something happens to change the heart. The wrath of God upon iniquity cannot be annulled as long as the causes of iniquity remain. Moral deterioration has no natural limit. Since life is continuous, all the spiritual consequences of sin continue forever.

Jesus also knew that a day of judgment is coming (Matt. 11:22; 12:36; Mark 6:11), when the direction of each person's life will be fixed. In that day the wicked will be severed from the just (Matt. 13:49; cf. 24:40; Luke 17:34), like a shepherd divides his sheep from the goats (Matt. 25:32, 46) or like wheat is separated from the tares (Matt. 13:30). Those who follow the course of this world will be told to "depart" from the presence of the Lord (Matt. 7:23; 24:41); they will be "cast out" (Matt. 8:12; 22:13; 25:30; Luke 13:28), "cursed" of God (Matt. 25:41), and assigned to "everlasting punishment" (Matt. 25:46).

That Jesus deeply felt this impending calamity of the lost is evidenced by His frequent reference to hell (Matt. 5:22, 29, 30; 10:28; 18:9; 23:15, 33; Mark 9:43, 45, 47; Luke 12:5).[9] The language used to describe it trembles with agony. Only by comparing His word pictures with experience within our mental grasp can we begin to comprehend its horror. Jesus called it a "place of torment" (Luke 16:23, 28) in which there shall be weeping, wailing, and gnashing of teeth (Matt. 8:12; 13:42, 50; 22:13; 24:51; 25:30). It is a state of pain characterized by fire that can neither be ignored nor forgotten—the fire of hell (Matt. 18:9 NIV), "a furnace of fire" (Matt. 13:42, cf. 40), "eternal fire prepared for the devil and his angels" (Matt. 25:41 RSV), "where decay never stops and the fire never goes out" (Mark 9:48 PHILLIPS; cf. 44, 46). Every vestige of good is

---

[9] The word *hell* (γέεννα), used by Jesus eleven times, as distinct from the word *hades* (ᾅδης), is equated with the Hebrew word *Gehenna*, (גיהבם), denoting a place of perpetual separation from God. A simple presentation of these concepts will be found in Leslie H. Woodson, *Hell and Salvation* (Old Tappan, N.J.: Fleming H. Revell, 1973), pp. 17–27.

gone. The soul is left in the terrifying loneliness of "outer darkness" forever (Matt. 8:12; 22:13; 25:30). Although the details are not elaborated, it would be impossible to project an image of hell any more dreadful than that portrayed by our Lord.

Is God Just?

Some will object to this teaching on the ground that it runs counter to God's nature of love. If there is punishment for sin beyond this life, they reason, it is remedial, not retributive, and, therefore, ultimately all erring children will be reformed.[10] In fairness to this position, it should be said that the thought of an eternal hell for the wicked is painful to accept. Certainly the Christian wishes it were not so. Even when convinced of the impossibility of the wicked gaining entrance into heaven, still as a duty of love, he desires the salvation of all.

What may be overlooked is that no one has suffered more in the contemplation of this human calamity than Jesus Himself. The cross is His witness.[11] Without destroying man's right to choose, God has done all He can to save man from sin, finally even giving Himself to die for us. It is the defiance of this love, the trampling under foot of the blood of Christ, that makes judgment inevitable.

---

[10] First advocated by Origen in the third century, and intermittently reappearing through the centuries, this view has received new impetus in recent years through the rise of modern existential and ecumenical theology. Such thinking confuses the eternity and unity of God's nature by not keeping His love in consistency with His holiness and justice. It also has the effect of undermining evangelistic concern. In this regard, a succinct statement on universalism is by Leslie Woodson, op. cit., pp. 29–108; a more complete treatment is Ajith R. Fernando's unpublished Master of Theology thesis at Fuller Theological Seminary (1976), entitled "A Critique of Exegetical Arguments for Universalism."

[11] The biblically astute Lewis Sperry Chafer observes: "If eternal punishment cannot be comprehended, it should be remembered that infinite holiness and the sin by which infinite holiness is outraged are equally unmeasurable by the human mind. God is not revealed as one who causes good people to suffer in hell, but He is revealed as one who at infinite cost has wrought to the end that sinners, believing on Christ, may not perish, but have everlasting life." *Major Bible Themes* (Grand Rapids: Zondervan, 1926), pp. 298, 299.

George Macdonald once remarked to C. S. Lewis: "There are only two kinds of people in the end, those who say to God, 'Thy will be done,' and those to whom God says, '*Thy* will be done.' All that are in hell chose it."[12] Not only is it man's choice, hell is the continual consequence of that rebellion. That is why it is so terrible. Hell is the place where sin, unrestrained by grace, develops its full potential in unending torment.

Call to Repentance

Knowing the impending doom, Jesus called men everywhere to turn from their course of destruction. Unless they forsake their evil way, they will all perish, like the Galileans "whose blood Pilate had mingled with their sacrifices" (Luke 13:1, 3), or those "upon whom the tower in Siloam fell" (Luke 13:4). There was an urgency in His voice, for the day of mercy was coming to an end.

Again and again this note was sounded in His teaching. The unfruitful tree would soon be cut down (Luke 13:6–9). Everyone bidden to the wedding feast must put on the proper garments, otherwise they will be driven out into the dark (Matt. 22:1–14). When the Bridegroom comes, those whose lamps are full of oil may enter into the banquet hall, but then the doors will be irrevocably shut (Matt. 25:1–12; cf. Luke 14:15–24).

Jesus wants men to heed God's call before the day of opportunity is gone (Luke 12:58, 59; Matt. 5:24, 26). Every person finally has to choose one of two alternatives—the broad way of the world, or the narrow way of life (Matt. 7:13, 14). Neutrality is not possible. Whether he likes it or not, man is building his house upon the sand, to perish; or upon the rock, to endure (Matt. 7:24–27).

The way of deliverance is to repent, meaning a complete change of direction.[13] It is closely akin to the idea of conver-

---

[12] C. S. Lewis, *The Great Divorce* (New York: Macmillan, 1946), p. 69.

[13] The verb *repent* ($\mu\epsilon\tau\alpha\nu o\acute{\epsilon}\omega$) occurs fifteen times in the words of Jesus (Matt. 4:17; 11:20, 21; 12:41; Mark 1:15; 6:12; Luke 10:13; 11:32; 13:3, 5; 15:7, 10; 16:30; 17:3, 4); and the noun form ($\mu\epsilon\tau\acute{\alpha}\nu o\iota\alpha$) five times (Matt. 9:13; Mark 2:17; Luke 5:32; 15:7; 24:47). There are a

sion.[14] Repentance implies a sense of contrition for the great offense toward God (Luke 18:13) and, where others are involved, a confession of the wrong toward them. This includes the desire to make things right (Matt. 5:23–25; Luke 17:4; 19:8). Jesus expected the rich young ruler to give up the worship of mammon (Mark 10:21; Matt. 19:21; Luke 18:22); the self-righteous lawyer to abandon his pride (Luke 10: 25, 37); the adulterous woman to go and sin no more (John 8:11; cf. 5:14).

In turning from the old patterns, the penitent soul is introduced to an entirely new life-style. The clean house is under new management. Jesus is Master. No longer will man seek to gratify his own selfish lusts. His desire is only to please his Lord and to live in obedience to the Father's will. Apart from this childlike humility no one can enter the Kingdom of Heaven (Matt. 18:3, 4).

Living by Faith

It is finally a question of faith. In whom does man place his confidence? Repentance is necessary, to be sure, but one has to believe the good news to be saved (Mark 1:15).[15] "In very truth," Jesus stated, "anyone who gives heed to what I say and

---

few other references in the Gospels to the term in John the Baptist's preaching. The basic idea is to change one's mind or purpose, implying moral action, and a resolution of amendment. There is an abhorrence of one's past, with a determination to enter upon a better course of life. Thayer, op. cit., pp. 405, 406. The word $\mu\epsilon\tau\alpha\mu\epsilon\lambda\mu\alpha\iota$, meaning remorse, used twice by Jesus (Matt. 21:29, 32), also carries the idea of repentance, though with more of an emotional overtone (Matt. 27:3; 2 Cor. 7:8; Heb. 7:21). See Kittel, IV, op. cit., pp. 625–629.

[14] The word is $\sigma\tau\rho\epsilon\phi\omega$ or $\epsilon\pi\iota\sigma\tau\rho\epsilon\phi\omega$, meaning to turn around or towards and often used in reference to spiritual experience, as in Matt. 13:15; 18:3; Mark 4:12; Luke 1:16, 17; 22:32; John 20:14, 16; also, Acts 3:19; 9:35, et al.

[15] The word *believe* in its various forms (chiefly $\pi\iota\sigma\tau\epsilon\upsilon\omega$, "to have faith," "to believe," "to rely on"; $\pi\iota\sigma\tau\iota\varsigma$, "faith," "trust," "belief"; and $\pi\iota\sigma\tau\sigma\varsigma$, "faithful," "trustworthy," "reliable") occurs over 160 times in the Gospels. About two-thirds are in John, underscoring the theme of the book as noted in John 20:30, 31. Consulting some good lexicons and dictionaries in reference to these terms will bring rich reward.

puts his trust in him who sent me has hold of eternal life, and does not come up for judgement, but has already passed from death to life" (John 5:24 NEB: cf. 11:25; 12:46, 47; 20:31, et al.). "No one who is alive and has faith shall ever die. Do you believe this?" Jesus asked (John 11:26 NEB). The issue is simple. Those who believe Christ will live; those who refuse will die in their sin (John 8:24).[16]

Faith in the Son of God is thus the condition of salvation. By this is meant a firm reliance upon His Word (John 2:22; 3:36; 4:21; 5:46, 47; 8:40; 20:29, 31; Luke 24:25) and an appropriation of His power (John 2:11; 4:50; 12:46; 20:27, 29; Mark 5:28). This principle is illustrated by the centurion who, concerned for his servant's welfare, asked Jesus only to speak the word of healing. As a soldier who lived under orders, He knew that one in authority had to be obeyed. The Master was so impressed with this display of faith that He called it to the attention of His disciples (Matt. 8:5–13; Luke 7:1–19). Another example He mentioned is the Syrophoenician woman who broke in upon the Master's retreat in Tyre and persisted in her plea that He help her afflicted daughter. She knew that whatever Jesus said would be done and, on that assurance, she would not be denied (Matt. 15:21–28; Mark 7:24–30).

Such confidence rests upon the conviction, "full of joyful trust, that Jesus is the Messiah, the divinely appointed Author of eternal salvation in the Kingdom of God." [17] In its essence is a personal relationship with Christ (John 11:27; 20:31). The Master does not ask us to believe a creed, but to believe a Person. "Come unto me . . ." He says, "and I will give you rest. Take my yoke upon you, and learn of me . . ." (Matt. 11:28, 29). This is the beauty of Christian faith. Jesus offers us

---

[16] Unbelief in Christ becomes the epitome of sin, for it constitutes the denial of God's gracious Word, and makes redemption impossible. Hence, Jesus taught that the unbeliever is condemned already (John 3:18); he shall not see life (John 3:36); he shall perish (John 3:16); the wrath of God abides on him (John 3:36); and he shall be damned (Mark 16:16; cf. Titus 1:15; 2 Cor. 4:4; 2 Thess. 2:10–12; Rom. 11:20; Heb. 3:18; 1 John 5:10; Rev. 21:8). Not surprisingly, then, the Holy Spirit's conviction of sin centers upon not believing Christ (John 16:9; cf. Rom. 14:23).

[17] Thayer, op. cit., p. 511.

Himself. "If any man thirst, let him come unto me, and drink" (John 7:37). "The man who comes to me I will never turn away" (John 6:37 NEB). "Come, take up the cross, and follow me" (Mark 10:21; Matt. 19:21; Luke 18:22; cf. John 1:43; Mark 1:17; 2:14; Matt. 4:19; 9:9; Luke 5:27).

This faith finds expression in action. It is a commitment of life. Many believed in the miracles of Christ, and acclaimed Him as a great teacher, but their hearts were not in it—their acceptance was merely an assent to historical fact, and Jesus did not trust Himself to them (John 2:23, 24; cf. 6:65, 66; 12:13–19). To believe on Christ is to come to Him (John 5:40; 6:35, 37, 40, 47, 65; 7:37); to receive Him (John 1:12; 5:42); to love Him supremely (John 8:42; 13:34; 14:28; 15:12; 16:27), which in its living demonstration becomes obedience to His commandments (John 8:31, 32, 42; 14:15, 21, 23, 25). In practice faith can never be separated from discipleship.

The Good News

The invitation is to all. God wants no one to perish (Matt. 18:14; cf. 2 Pet. 3:9; 1 Tim. 2:4). True, no man can come to Christ "except it were given unto him" of the Father (John 6:65; cf. 6:37; 17:2, 24), but whoever believes will receive the gift.[18] This is the Gospel Jesus came to proclaim—incredible to the spiritually blind (John 8:47; 9:27; 10:26; 18:37)—but the wisdom and power of God to those of a believing heart. "For God so loved the world that he gave his one and only Son, that whoever believes in him shall not perish but have everlasting life" (John 3:16 NIV: cf. 1:7).

What makes the message so difficult for the worldly wise to accept is that it completely circumvents the world's system of

---

[18] The sovereign will of God and Man's freedom of choice are both underscored in Scripture. Reconciling the two truths surpasses human understanding. But of this we can be sure: God draws, man responds. The whole movement of redemption, from beginning to end, is initiated by divine grace. Man's part is simply to let God have His way. Hence, salvation is entirely God's act to the praise of His eternal glory; while separation from grace is due completely to man's willful hardness of heart. A good discussion of this issue may be found in J. I. Packer, *Evangelism and the Sovereignty of God* (Downers Grove, Illinois: InterVarsity Press, 1961).

earning favor. Since all men are morally bankrupt, estranged from God and each other, and under the sentence of death, no one can be saved through good works. Only as God shows mercy is there any hope. If we got justice, everyone would be consigned to hell. We can understand why the chief priests and elders were scandalized at such preaching, for it actually put known "sinners," like the publicans and harlots, in a better position to believe the Gospel than they themselves (Matt. 21:28–32).

God's good news is that Jesus has borne our judgment that we might receive His grace. Salvation is the free gift of God received by faith in Christ alone. We are without merit, yet Jesus promises the forgiveness of sins (Matt. 9:2, 5, 6; Mark 2:5, 9, 10; Luke 5:21; 7:49); the believing soul is at peace. Every person who walks by faith no longer stumbles in darkness, but has the light of unfading truth shining in the inner man (John 1:4; 8:12; 12:35, 46); death loses its hold (John 11:25; Luke 15:32); the spirit is free (John 8:36). In this liberty, the commandments are embraced with gladness, and love fills obedience with heavenly praise.

This is the life Jesus came to give the world—the life He experienced—true life, abundant life, eternal life (Luke 18:30; John 4:36; 6:40, 47; 10:10; 17:3; 20:31, et al.). Breathtaking in its scope! Unsearchable in its glory! And it is given to all who receive Him, "even to those that believe on his name" (John 1:12). Such are the children of God—children "not born of any human stock, or by fleshly desire of a human father, but the offspring of God himself" (John 1:13 NEB).

With this knowledge of the Gospel, Jesus could not be casual about evangelism. Man had to hear the Word of Life, or there was no way of reconciliation. One can understand why His eyes filled with tears when He looked out upon Jerusalem (Luke 19:41–44). He saw that the people did not know those things which belonged to their peace, and their time for salvation was coming to an end. Nevertheless, He could not abandon them, and as long as He had strength, He ceased not to tell the Good News of God's redeeming grace (Luke 20:1).

The Challenge Today

So it is with all who would follow in His steps. Knowing man's potential, both for good and evil, we cannot be indifferent to the Gospel mandate. Eternal destinies are at stake. Heaven and hell are in the balance. If we do not evangelize, we in effect abandon men to utter despair and doom.

The Christian lives like one who has been rescued from a burning city. He is overwhelmed with the wonder of being saved, yet broken at the thought of loved ones left behind. Familiarity with grace must never deaden our sensibility to the multitudes still in bondage. We might be tempted to think that by their affection for the world they are unworthy of consideration, seeing they crucify Christ afresh. But we must remember that they, too, are persons for whom Jesus died, "and do for them what we would have them do for us if we were in their place." [19] In fact, by God's grace, they not only can receive illumination, but may soon acquire more faith than we ourselves.

Of this we may be assured: However great the strength of sin, the redeeming power of God is greater. We must make it known—clearly, unequivocally, the Gospel must be heralded across the earth. Here every disciple of Christ has responsibility. Would that we could sense the urgency of Wesley when he said: "Give me one hundred preachers who fear nothing but sin and desire nothing but God, and I care not a straw whether they be clergymen or laymen, such alone will shake the gates of hell and set up the kingdom of heaven on earth." [20]

---

[19] Blaise Pascal, *Pensées*, trans. H. F. Stewart (London: Rutledge and Kegan Paul, 1950), p. 111.
[20] John Wesley, *The Letters of the Reverend John Wesley*, ed. John Telford, VI (London: The Epworth Press, 1931), p. 272.

For this cause came I into the world.
John 18:37

5

His Way of the Cross

Jesus' knowledge of the Gospel included far more than understanding man's need; He realized what was required of His own life to make the Gospel a reality. To probe what this means brings us into the very heartbeat of our Lord's ministry.

Sent to Redeem

Jesus lived under a mandate from God. Again and again He emphasized: "I came down from heaven, not to do mine own will, but the will of him that sent me" (John 6:38); "I have not come on my own; but he sent me" (John 8:42 NIV).[1] This was His daily fare, as He said: "My meat is to do the will of him that sent me, and to finish his work" (John 4:34; cf. 3:34; 6:57; 7:16; 12:49; 17:18, 26).

The assignment was the redemption of mankind. To use His words, "For I did not come to judge the world, but to save it" (John 12:47 NIV; cf. 3:17). This was the purpose for His physical existence—the reason He threw off the robes of glory, and clothed Himself with our flesh. He knew that the Son of Man

---

[1] Nearly sixty times in the Gospels Jesus refers to Himself in this manner. The words used are about evenly divided between πέμπω, "to send," as with purpose (e.g., Luke 20:13; John 1:33; 4:34; 5:23, 24, 30, 37; 6:38, 39, 40, 44; 7:16, 18, 28, 33; 8:16, 18, 26, 29; 9:4; 12:44, 45, 49; 13:16, 20; 14:24, 26; 15:21, 26 [The Holy Spirit]; 16:5, 7), and ἀποστέλλω, "to send," as on an official mission (Matt. 10:40; 15:24; Mark 9:37; Luke 4:18, 43; 9:48; 10:16; John 3:17, 34; 5:38; 6:29, 57; 7:29; 8:42; 10:36; 11:42; 17:3, 8, 18, 21, 23, 25; 20:21). Both verbs are also frequently applied to His disciples, underscoring the similarity of their missions.

was come to seek and to save the lost (Luke 19:10; cf. Ezk. 34:11–16).

Illustrative of this self-consciousness, Jesus referred to Himself as a shepherd going after wandering sheep (Luke 15:4; cf. Mark 14:27; Matt. 26:31; John 10:1–18); and the door of the sheepfold through which all who will be saved must enter (John 10:9). To the sin-sick soul, He is the healing physician (Matt. 9:12; Mark 2:17; Luke 5:31); to those walking in darkness, He is the light of men (John 1:4; 8:12; 9:5; 12:35, 46); to multitudes starving for spiritual food, He is the living bread (John 6:50–58); to a world languishing in despair, He is the bringer of good tidings (Matt. 11:5; Luke 3:18; 4:18, 43; 7:22; 8:1; 9:6; 16:16; 20:1).

One of the most graphic descriptions of His mission is the parable of the great supper, where the master of the house sent his servant out to announce that the feast was ready. When those first invited made excuses, the servant was sent to the streets and forgotten places where people live, seeking by every possible means of persuasion to bring them in (Luke 14:15–24; cf. Matt. 22:1–14). Such was the feeling in the heart of Jesus. He shared that compulsion to see God's table filled, and like the faithful servant, went forth to do the works of God "as long as it is day," for "night is coming, when no one can work" (John 9:4 NIV).

Emptying Himself

With this purpose always before Him, Jesus subordinated His natural human desires to the higher calling of God. This was a working day for Him. Anything which did not contribute to the salvation of men had no place in His life. He was not here to receive the plaudits of men; rather He came to minister, and to give His life as a ransom for others (Matt. 20:28; Mark 10:45).

Knowing this required the renunciation of His own rights, He stripped Himself of every divine advantage and "took upon him the form of a servant" (Phil. 2:7). This self-emptying of Jesus, called the *kenosis*, transcends all our attempts at explanation. For it means that the Prince of heaven, God's eternal Son, gave up His place of glory and subjected Himself to the most abject kind of servitude in order to become our Redeemer. Though He was rich, for our sake He became poor, that we who are so impoverished might partake of His riches (2 Cor. 8:9).

The servant role He chose was immediately apparent in the humble circumstances of His birth and childhood. Thirty years He lived in obscurity, growing up in a carpenter's home where austerity and hard labor were a matter of necessity. It is probable that Joseph died while Jesus was still a young man, leaving Him the responsibility as the eldest son to support His mother and brothers and sisters. He knew what it was to share the pangs of loved ones in need, and to bear the responsibility of keeping a home together. Doubtless those experiences intensified His sensitivity to human suffering, and show how God did not circumvent the slow, painful process of growth in accomplishing His mission. The silent years of learning were also part of the plan.

A Servant's Detachment

When Jesus at last set out on His public ministry, He trusted His livelihood and security to others. If He had any money, He apparently did not carry it with Him; at least, He had to borrow a penny to show the superscription of Caesar (Mark 12:15, 16; Matt. 22:19, 20; Luke 20:24; cf. John 13:29). Traveling about he country, He had no place to call His own (Matt. 8:20), but lived with friends and shared their hospitality (Mark 1:29; Luke 8:3; cf. Matt. 27:55, 56).[2] Even His tomb belonged to a friend (Matt. 27:57–60; Mark 15:43–46; Luke 23:50–53; John 19:38–42).

It should not be assumed, however, that Jesus was opposed to private ownership. He freely made use of the means of others, and always showed appreciation for their kindness.

---

[2] This arrangement offered a beautiful way for others to become involved in His ministry, while also providing for His needs. Besides, Jesus was unmarried, and it was ideally suited to His itinerant lifestyle. However, lest we take this pattern of Jesus literally, let me emphasize again the uniqueness of His situation. The principle of self-giving, of course, applies in any life, but the details will vary according to the circumstances.

Wealthy businessmen, centurions, noblemen, tax collectors
and members of the Sanhedrin were among His friends. There
is nothing inherently wrong with wealth, just as there is no
virtue in poverty. But Jesus warned against the danger of trusting in riches (Luke 6:24; 12:16–21; 16:9, 11; Matt. 6:19–21).
The temptation is to let mammon become an end in itself.
Those who succumb to this deception, like the rich young
ruler, have a harder time entering the Kingdom of God than a
camel has going through a needle's eye (Mark 10:24, 25; Matt.
19:24; Luke 18:25).[3] God's rule can have no rival in the heart
of man.

Living with this standard, of course, implies a radical revi-
sion of pagan values (Matt. 6:31, 32). The godly outlook involves more than mere detachment from material goods; it is
an attitude of indifference to fame and reputation, counting as
dross all those things which natural man holds dear. "Blessed
are the poor in spirit," He taught (Matt. 5:3; cf. Luke 6:20). No
longer anxious to possess treasures which moth and rust corrupt, such simple ones devote themselves to the spiritual
realities which cannot be taken from them. When one seeks
"first the kingdom of God, and his righteousness," he can be
assured that the other things will fall in place (Matt. 6:33).

Not of This World

This radical loyalty to God's dominion also had its effect in
Jesus' attitude toward the existent world system. Asked by the
Pharisees and Herodians, "Is it right for us to pay taxes to
Caesar or not?" Jesus answered: "Give to Caesar what is
Caesar's, and to God what is God's" (Matt. 22:17, 21; Mark
12:14, 17; Luke 20:22, 25 NIV). His reply refrains from either a
yes or a no, pointing to another alternative which lies beyond
both: Give to Caesar his due—money—for it belongs to him;

---

[3] An interesting aspect of this instruction is that the money was to
be given away to the poor, not to each other. Though the disciples
seem to have had a community fund from which they drew from time
to time (John 13:29), and later developed a concept of lovingly holding possessions in common (Acts 4:32), this is not remotely analogous
to modern systems of forced state socialism.

and give to God what is His right to possess—your whole being, body, mind, and soul.

Jesus advocated neither withdrawing from society nor evading support of the state. But He taught the disciples to get their spiritual citizenship clear.[4] Though they lived in the world, they did not belong to it (John 15:19; 17:14–16). His Kingdom is of a different order over and above creation (John 18:36). Those who follow Him live by the ethic of this higher government. They form a new community, however imperfectly realized now, within the existing culture of the world. In this way their lives separately and together demonstrate the true character of holiness. Like a city set on a hill, they expose the falsity of the world around them (Matt. 5:14).

This does not suggest passivity in the struggle against corruption, only a different strategy. The Gospels show Jesus, like the prophets before Him, relentlessly contending for social justice and brotherhood among men. He condemned the oppressors of the weak with startling directness. For this forthright stand, He was always in trouble with the ruling religious aristocracy, and finally He was denounced as a rebel (John 11:48).[5] Yet, to the great disappointment of the rev-

---

[4] Those who would like to explore this subject further, especially in its political and social ramifications, should read Marcel Clement, *Christ and Revolution*, trans. from the French by Alice von Hildebrand with Marilyn Teichert (New Rochelle, N.Y.: Arlington House, 1974); Oscar Cullman, *Jesus and the Revolutionaries*, trans. from the German by Gareth Putnam (New York: Harper and Row, 1970); and John Yoder, *The Politics of Jesus* (Grand Rapids: Wm. B. Eerdmans, 1972), replete with many other bibliographical references.

[5] The High Priest and the scribes called Jesus a blasphemer (Matt. 9:3; 26:65; Mark 14:64; John 10:33). He was described by the Pharisees as a glutton and a winebibber (Luke 7:33, 34); a lawbreaker (John 9:16; Mark 2:24; 7:2, 5); a tax dodger (Matt. 17:24); and a colleague of publicans and sinners (Matt. 9:10). The Jews called Him a liar (John 8:45); a deceiver (Matt. 27:63; cf. John 7:12, 47); a madman (John 10:20); and by implication, a bastard (John 8:40, 41). They accused Him of contemplating suicide (John 8:21, 22); and said He had a devil (Mark 3:22; John 7:20; 8:48, 49, 52). If the temple rulers could have found a way, they would have killed Him from the very first. As it was, they were continually scheming to put Him to death (John 8:37, 40, 59; 11:8, 53; cf. Luke 4:28).

olutionary Zealots, He led no crusade to forcefully overthrow the civil authority (cf. Matt. 10:34; 26:52; Luke 22:36, 48–51: John 18:11).[6]

His approach was far more radical—and realistic; He attacked the root of man's problem, not its symptoms. Without this basic conversion, any restructuring of society would be superficial. To be sure, just social systems promote the common good, and therefore should be sought. But all the governments of men, however good, are still under God's judgment and will perish. So whatever the system, the self-serving sinners in it need to become a part of that Kingdom where love motivates every desire. This is the kind of revolution Jesus came to lead.

Never Appreciated

Such a mission is never popular because it allows no compromise with sin. Selfish men, obsessed with materialism, naturally think of happiness in terms of fleshly indulgence. With such a perverted objective, it is easy to reason that the end justifies any means to its attainment. So it is not surprising that the people at last rejected Jesus. The Messiah they expected was to come as a mighty warrior who would triumph over Israel's enemies and establish an invincible empire on this earth. They could not visualize a Kingdom of the Spirit. Nor could they comprehend Christ's bringing the Kingdom to

---

[6] The Zealots were a fanatical faction within Judaism violently opposed to their Roman oppressors, who believed in the imminent coming of the Messianic rule. They would have been attracted to Jesus' teaching about the Kingdom being at hand, as well as His criticism of the Gentile rulers (Luke 13:32; 22:25). Some authorities, like S. G. F. Brandon in *Jesus and the Zealots* (Manchester: Manchester U.P., 1967), have suggested that Jesus was allied with this group. It is apparent that Simon, one of the Twelve, was a Zealot (Luke 6:15; Acts 1:13), though there is no indication that he remained one after following Jesus. Possibly, too, Peter "Barjona" and Judas Iscariot had an early association with this movement, suggested by Oscar Cullmann, op. cit., p. 9. Nevertheless, the whole tenor of Jesus' teaching, as well as His personal rejection of political aspirations, precluded any active support of the Zealot cause. Both their goals and methods were poles apart from His.

pass by suffering with humanity as the servant of God.[7] As long as He excited their physical expectations with His miraculous deeds, they wanted Him to be their king (John 6:15; cf. 3:26; 11:47, 48; 12:19). They lined the highway, shouting "Hosanna! Blessed is he who comes in the name of the Lord! Blessed is the King of Israel!" (John 12:13 NIV; cf. Mark 11:9, 10; Matt. 21:9; Luke 19:38). It looked like the world had gone after Him (John 12:19; cf. Mark 12:12; Matt. 21:26; Luke 20:19). But when it became apparent that He was not the Messiah they expected, the fickle crowds, manipulated by their embittered leaders, cried out "Crucify him; crucify him!" (John 19:6 RSV; cf. Mark 15:13; Matt. 27:22; Luke 23:21).[8]

If Jesus had only accommodated Himself to their natural appetites, the multitudes would have been at His feet (John 12:19; cf. Mark 12:12; Matt. 21:26; Luke 20:19), and the cross could have been avoided. Certainly with His power it would have been nothing for Jesus to overthrow the corrupt governments of His day. He could have set Himself upon the throne of the world. Was not this His temptation in the wilderness?

---

[7] For a concise statement of the popular expectation of the Messiah in Jesus' time, see Oscar Cullmann, op. cit., p. 38. He believes that the people's misunderstanding of the Messiah's role explains why Jesus observed such restraint toward the term when it is conferred on Him.

[8] It might be argued that this was a different crowd than was present when Jesus rode into the city. Perhaps so, but still one would have to ask where those multitudes were that had shouted His praises a few days before. Lest we be too hard on them, however, let us remember that most of the people Jesus befriended along the way also turned back from following Him when it became apparent that He was not the Messiah they expected (John 6:60–66). His own brothers and sisters in the family of Joseph could not understand Him (John 7:2–6). Even those few disciples that stayed with Him were steeped in the thinking of their self-centered culture and found it hard to accept His redemptive teaching and example. They did not want Jesus to die. That He would suffer humiliation and rejection by their nation seemed impossible (e.g., Matt. 16:22, 23; Mark 8:31, 32; Luke 9:22, 23). When at last the night descended, and He was taken away to be tried and condemned, they all panicked and fled (Matt. 26:56, 31; Mark 14:27, 50–52).

(Matt. 4:1–7; Luke 4:1–13). That He viewed the suggestion as a Satanic deception poses a bewildering problem for those activists who see His mission only in terms of social and political reformation.

Works of Compassion

Yet, on the personal level, the Master continuously ministered to the physical sufferings of humanity. He moved among them "as one who serves" (Luke 22:27 RSV; cf. John 13:4, 5). With compassion (Matt. 20:34; Mark 1:41; Luke 7:13; John 11:35), He fed the hungry, healed the sick, made the lame walk, gave hearing to the deaf, cleansed the lepers, opened the eyes of the blind, cast out demons, and raised the dead. Day after day He lived the role of a ministering servant, giving unstintingly of Himself to alleviate suffering about Him.

His works reflected the miraculous quality of His life.[9] The power of God flowed through them. In a way which the people could see, they attested to His divine relationship with the Father, showed His supremacy over Satan, and called attention to His authoritative Word. Thus, His works confirmed His teaching, so that what He did brought men to believe in Him (John 10:25, 38; 14:11; 15:24). This was the witness that God had sent Him (John 5:36; 6:29; 10:25; 11:42; 17:8, 21, 23, 25; Matt. 11:2–6; Luke 7:18–23).[10]

---

[9] There are at least forty miracles recorded in the Gospels, all in some way meeting human need. Most relate to physical healing. Jesus did not exploit illness and tragedy to display His power, but He made it an occasion to draw men into the Kingdom. For a discussion of the miracles of Christ, see A. B. Bruce, *The Miraculous Element in the Gospels* (New York: George H. Doran, 1886); John Laidlaw, *The Miracles of Our Lord* (London: Hodder and Stoughton, 1890), Richard Chenevix Trench, *Notes on the Miracles of Our Lord* (London: Kegan Paul, Trench, Trübner, and Co., 1911); and the most thorough recent study by H. Van Der Loos, *The Miracles of Jesus* (Leiden: E. J. Brill, 1965). An excellent bibliography is included in the latter.

[10] The same disposition toward truth which made the teachings of Christ relevant to spiritually sensitive persons also applied to His deeds. Those who were hardened in heart could not interpret the works of Christ with any more understanding than His Word (e.g., John 15:22–25). Unfortunately, most people who saw the miracles of

His compassion knew no barriers of culture, race, sex, class, or age. Beggars, lowly women, and slaves received the same consideration as merchants, lawyers, and priests. He was especially mindful of those persons largely forgotten by society. Hence, widows, orphans, and sojourners, along with the poor, were objects of His special care.[11]

In the same way, Jesus expected the disciples to authenticate their testimony. They were to demonstrate their love for Him by loving those He loved—including the hungry, the thirsty, the stranger, the naked, the sick, and the prisoner—"As you did it to one of the least of these my brethren, you did it to me" (Matt. 25:40 RSV; cf. 10:42; John 21:16). His appeals to give unsparingly to the poor reflected the same practical concern (Luke 12:33; Mark 10:21; Matt. 6:4, 2). In Jesus' teaching, everyone according to ability has a social obligation to his fellowman. Welfare programs of the state do not absolve the Christian from the necessity of personal involvement. Nor can one believe God for supernatural assistance until he has exhausted the available natural means of help. Just as freely as we have received, we should gratefully give to others as unto the Lord. Self-giving is the measure of greatness in His Kingdom. "Whosoever will be great among you, shall be your minister," He said, "And whosoever of you will be the chiefest, shall be servant of all" (Mark 10:43, 44; cf. Luke 10:36, 37; John 13:14).[12]

Jesus interpreted them in terms of their materialistic, self-centered interests, like the people who believed in Him simply because they had been fed (John 6:26). Others clamored for more "signs" of His power, not because they wanted to follow Him, but because such displays appealed to their fleshly appetites.

[11] Jesus' attitude in this respect reflects the Old Testament ethic whereby God is the protector of persons who had no legal standing among men. Those who violated these persons were answerable to Him. It is God's character which ultimately commands social compassion. Neither humanitarian concern nor a sense of righteousness, in itself, is adequate to sustain genuine love for the rejects of society. Humanitarian efforts apart from the love of God soon fizzle, or else degenerate into legalism, or worse, despotism.

[12] Note John Stott's definition of the word *mission*, particularly his distinction between the great commission and the great commandment of Jesus. He sees social action as "a partner of evangelism." They share the same mandate of love, yet are independent of each

The Spoken Word

The ministry of Christ, however, included more than service to the physical needs of humanity. Man must understand his spiritual birthright in God's plan. The compassionate works of Jesus attracted people to Him, but they did not explain the reason for His presence in the world. If He had lived among us only as a doer of good deeds, doubtless He would have been regarded as the most selfless example of love who ever lived, yet still we would die in our sins without eternal life. His redemptive mission was not clear until He articulated the Gospel.

So in His servant role Jesus was constantly explaining the grace of God in relation to man's spiritual needs. Healing was invariably linked with preaching and teaching (Matt. 4:23; 9:35; 10:7, 8; Luke 4:18, 19; 9:6). His mission to the world was inseparable from witnessing to the truth (John 18:37). Wherever He went along the highways, in market places, before tax offices, walking through cemeteries, at public wells, on seashores, in the synagogues, and within private homes—He was talking about the Kingdom of God. Sometimes in the larger gatherings His message sounded forth like a fanfare of trumpets announcing the coming of a king.[13] More often, however, He was a teacher quietly instructing the persons

---

other. The reason we show concern about the welfare of people's bodies and relationships is not to give the Gospel "visibility or credibility it would otherwise lack," but rather because "love expresses itself in service wherever it sees need." *Christian Mission in the Modern World*, pp. 27, 30. For a good treatment of the service concept of ministry, see Gabriel Fackre, *Word in Deed* (Grand Rapids: Wm. B. Eerdmans, 1975).

[13] The word commonly translated "preach" ($\kappa\eta\rho\acute{\upsilon}\sigma\sigma\omega$) conveys the idea of declaring an authoritative message. It is associated with the office of a herald ($\kappa\hat{\eta}\rho\upsilon\xi$), whose duty it was to lift up his voice and declare official decrees. Sometimes he would use a trumpet to gather the people. The essential point about such a person is that "behind his message stands a higher power: the herald does not express his own views. He is the spokesman for his master." Kittel, op. cit., III, p. 688; note the whole article, pp. 683–714. When used in the New Testament, this strong sense of proclaiming the Word of Another—God—comes into preaching. It is used in reference to Jesus in Matthew 4:17, 23; 9:35; 11:1; Mark 1:14, 38, 39, 45; 5:20; 6:12; Luke 4:18, 19, 44; 8:1; and is used by Jesus or others in reference to His

around Him.[14] The most common words describing His manner of speech mean "to converse"—just plain, ordinary discourse. It was as natural as it was unceasing.[15] One could not have been around Him long without hearing the Gospel.

Reflecting this style, Jesus was essentially a personal evangelist. Though thousands came to hear Him (Matt. 14:21; 15:38; Mark 6:44; 8:9; John 6:10), these public gatherings were not the source of His greatest victories. Doubtless they served to introduce multitudes to the Gospel, and thereby prepared hearts to receive Him. But the real impact of His message came in person-to-person dialogue as He went about His daily work.[16]

He appeared utterly confident and at ease. Nothing was staged or forced, nor was anyone coerced to make a decision. Rather He bore witness to the truth, identifying God's Word in the world. He was content to let the Holy Spirit apply it to their hearts, without undue anxiety about the tabulation of results.

---

disciples in Matthew 10:1, 27; 24:14; 26:13; Mark 3:14; 7:36; 13:10; 14:9; 16:15, 20; Luke 8:39; 9:2; 12:3; 24:47. The noun *preacher* or *herald* is not used in the Gospels, but is found in 1 Timothy 2:7; 2 Timothy 1:11 and 2 Peter 2:5. The word *evangelize*, as previously noted, also implies proclamation, and is used in connection with κηρύσσω in Luke 8:1, and the noun form *Gospel* in Matthew 4:23; 9:35; 26:13; Mark 13:10; 14:9; and 16:15.

[14] The usual word διδάσκω, meaning "to teach" or "to give instruction," is used about fifty times in reference to Jesus; and He is called διδάσκαλος (a teacher or master) almost as often.

[15] Various words are used in this capacity, principally λέγω or λαλέω, all of which carry the idea of normal talking. They describe Jesus' way of communication hundreds of times.

[16] The methodology of Jesus in personal evangelism falls outside the scope of this study. However, the subject is treated by many authors, including William P. Barber, Raymond Calkins, George Cornell, John Hunter, C. E. Macartney, F. V. McFatridge, James McConaughy, L. R. Scarborough, John Sligh, John Smith, Ernest Clyde Wareing, to mention a few. Perhaps the best exegetical work, covering the wide range of personalities in the Gospels, is G. Campbell Morgan, *The Great Physician* (Old Tappan N.J.: Fleming H. Revell, 1972, © 1937). An inductive study of the most prominent of these personal confrontations is my *They Meet the Master* (Fort Lauderdale: Christian Outreach, 1973). The bibliography in this book lists ample materials for further study.

Call to Follow

As already noted, those who believed were expected to follow Him. One did not have to know very much to take the first step, but he had to be willing to learn; that is, to become His disciple. Though the depth of commitment was open-ended, implied in the response was the conviction that Jesus Christ is Lord.

The Master devoted Himself to the training of these followers who formed a counterculture of righteousness in the midst of paganism. From this growing fellowship, He selected twelve of the most alert disciples for special attention, though within this group, Peter, James, and John had an even closer association. This was the nucleus around which He built a Church. While He continued His ministry to the masses, He concentrated upon these men who would someday lead the others.

To show what this leadership meant, Jesus brought His disciples close to Himself, so close that they could feel the pulse of His life and experience firsthand His mission to the world. For the better part of three years they walked the trails together; they observed His priorities unfolding in disciplined devotion; they were with Him as He reached out to minister to the body and soul of the heavy laden; they saw His love in action every day. Though their comprehension of His spiritual objective was painfully slow, gradually by following Him they learned what He was in the world to do and how He did it.

The deliberate way that He went about discipling men can only be viewed as an essential ingredient of His life's purpose. It did not happen accidentally. Though the working of the plan seems quite natural, it must have been carefully calculated by Jesus. This was His program for world evangelization. Everything else depended upon it, for if His disciples did not learn to perpetuate His life and teaching, then His coming into the world would be in vain.

Obedient Unto Death

As His ministry lengthened, Jesus often spoke of His death, the references becoming more pronounced as He neared the end.[17] He was keenly aware that the Gospel He lived and preached had to be sealed in blood. This had been determined in the mind of God before the stars were fixed in place (Rev. 13:8; cf. Acts 2:23). There was no other way that men under the sentence of death could be reconciled to the Father. The Lamb of God had to die for the sins of mankind.

So from the beginning Jesus set His face toward Calvary. He was not the victim of foul circumstance, caught in a plot over which He had no control. This was the moment for which He was born (John 2:4; 7:6; 12:27; 17:1; 18:37). Jesus raised the question Himself, "Shall I ask the Father to save Me from death?" (a paraphrase). Then, to show the error of this way of thinking, He answered: "No, it was for this very reason I came to this hour" (John 12:27, NIV). He did not plan on missing the crowning event of His life. Continually dedicating Himself to this purpose constituted His sanctification—the setting Himself apart to God for our sake (John 17:19; cf. 18:36).[18] The Jews killed His reputation, and the Romans crucified His body, but Jesus offered up His life on the cross. "No one takes it from me," He explained, "I lay it down of my own accord" (John 10:18 NIV).

The determination not to be diverted from His mission comes into climactic focus in the Garden of Gethsemane. There, "overwhelmed with sorrow to the point of death" (Matt. 26:38 NIV), Jesus saw the Father holding a cup before Him. It expressed in some mysterious way the intense suffering of this hour when He bore alone the anguish of a lost world. As such, the physical torture of the cross, later to be endured, was only an outward display of the mental and

---

[17] The Gospels record Jesus alluding to His death at least sixteen times prior to His crucifixion. It does not appear that the disciples grasped what He meant until the very end. A listing of these references will be found in *The Master Plan of Evangelism*, pp. 53, 54.

[18] The word *sanctify*, coming from a root meaning "to set apart," is often applied to persons who are dedicated for a special work (e.g., Jer. 1:5; 2 Chron. 26:18; Eccles. 45:4; Acts 20:32; 26:18; Heb. 2:11). In both John 17:19, where Jesus speaks of sanctifying Himself, and in John 10:36, where the agent of His consecration is the Father, the reference is to the mission for which He was sent into the world. For a discussion of this verse, see J. H. Bernard, *A Critical and Exegetical Commentary in the Gospel According to John*, ed. A. H. McNeile, II (Edinburgh: T. & T. Clark, 1963, © 1928), pp. 369, 575; also *The Master Plan of Evangelism*, pp. 63, 64.

spiritual anguish of His soul. In His human fraility He asked
that the cup might be taken from Him; nevertheless, realizing
there was no other way for His task to be completed, He drank
the cup to its dregs, and hurled it forth in victory (Matt.
26:36–46; Mark 14:32–42; Luke 22:39–46).[19] There was no
hesitancy or anxiety in His voice as He awoke His sleeping
disciples with the words: "Let us be going" (Matt. 26:46;
Mark 14:42). However great the suffering, He knew that His
steps were directed by One who never makes mistakes.[20]

He lived in obedience; He died in obedience. The things
He suffered were only means of teaching Him more about
obedience (Heb. 5:8). In this sense, the cross displays a life
totally obedient to the will of God. Jesus always did those
things which the Father commanded (John 8:28, 55; 14:31;
17:4), thereby permitting God to perfect His purpose in
human flesh.

Constraining Love

But we miss the motivation for Christ's sacrifice if we see it
solely as a result of duty. There was that necessity, to be sure,
but the obedience was constrained by love—that benevolent
nature of God in Christ which ever seeks the good of its beloved, that is always giving itself away. Such love knows no
bounds; it asks not how little, but how much. "No one has
greater love than the one who lays down his life for his
friends" (John 15:13 NIV; cf. John 3:16; 1 John 3:16; 4:8).

The cross then reveals what Jesus meant when He told His

[19] Some interpret these words to mean that Jesus felt so deeply the
burden of the world that He was afraid He might die under its weight
in the Garden, and not live to offer the sacrifice. Accordingly, it is
believed, He was asking the Father to give Him strength to complete
His work on the cross. This view may accent even more the sense of
His mission, though in either explanation we see humanity in perfect
conformity to the will of God.

[20] Pascal, in his penetrating description of our Lord's agony in
Gethsemane, observes that "Jesus, while His disciples slept,
wrought their salvation. He has wrought that of each of the righteous
while they slept, both in their nothingness before their birth, and in
their sins after their birth . . . Jesus, seeing all His friends asleep
and all His enemies wakeful, commits Himself entirely to His
Father . . . . If God gave us masters by His own hand, Oh! how
necessary for us to obey them with a good heart! Necessity and
events follow infallibly." *Pensées*, ed. Sutton, op. cit., p. 149.

disciples to remain in His love, "even as I have kept my Father's commandments, and abide in his love" (John 15:10; cf. 15:9, 10; 14:21–24). It is an appeal to actively conform to the will of God, not out of coercion but because it is the desire of our hearts. This was the secret of Jesus' joy, and He covets the same experience for His disciples (John 15:11).[21] Hence, He calls them "friends" (John 15:15). A servant does not know his master's business; he knows only the command to act. But a friend knows not only the command, but the reason behind it.

Borne along by this knowledge of God's motive, the Christian ministry is a labor of love. Such love springs irresistibly from the enraptured soul of one who knows that Christ "loved me and gave himself for me" (Gal. 2:20 RSV; cf. 2 Cor. 5:14). That is why, however difficult the work, the Christian does not complain in adversity nor carry resentment when unappreciated. For the obedient follower of Christ never seeks himself, but seeks only the glory of his Lord in all things. Any work motivated by this kind of devotion is pleasing to the Master. As one has reminded us: "God weighs more with how much love a man works than how much he does. He does much who loves much." [22]

Taking Up Our Cross

Let no one be misled, however. Love is costly. It cost Jesus His life. And it will cost ours, too, if we take His work to our heart. The worldlings who mocked Jesus at the cross were correct when they jeered: "He saved others; himself he cannot save" (Matt. 27:42; Mark 15:31; Luke 23:35). What they failed to understand is that Jesus was not in the world to save Himself; He was here to save us. No one can finally save himself and still fulfill the mission of God.

This is the decision we must make in answering the summons of the Master to "take up his cross," and follow Him (Matt. 16:24; Mark 8:34; Luke 9:23; cf. Matt. 19:21; Mark 10:21; Luke 14:27–33). The call is to renounce our own rights in loving submission to His lordship. There is the sense in

---

[21] Again Pascal succinctly speaks to the point: "Self-will will never be satisfied, though it should have command of all it would; but we are satisfied from the moment we renounce it. Without it we cannot be discontented; with it we cannot be content." Ibid., p. 131.

[22] Thomas á Kempis, op. cit., p. 24.

which every servant of Christ must drink of His cup and take of His baptism (John 18:11; Luke 12:49, 50). Self-assertion must die. Obedience is never final until there is a cross.

Once settled, the commitment must be continually confirmed by the renewing of our mind. "No man, having put his hand to the plow, and looking back, is fit for the kingdom of God" (Luke 9:62). Our call is to martyrdom, for only then are we free to serve Him in that love with which we are loved.[23] This is the paradox of the cross. By losing our life for the sake of the Gospel we not only discover the joy of Christ's life, but we also learn how God can work through us (Matt. 16:25; 19:29; Mark 8:35). Except a grain of wheat fall to the earth and die, it cannot bring forth fruit (John 12:24).

The Sacrificial Life

It is well enough to understand the theological significance of this truth, but it is more important for us to incarnate its meaning in daily life. Here I suspect most of us feel a bit uneasy. For whatever our experience may be, in light of what Christ has done for us, any sacrifice that we make for Him is hardly worthy of the name.

Certainly the cross urges us to get our objectives clearly established. We are sent into the world, not to satisfy our own whims of ambition, but to do the will of Him who commands us. For us the cross does not mean that we will die for the world. That has been done by Jesus. But in accepting the benefit of His vicarious death, we are made aware that we are no longer our own, and compelled by the mandate of His love,

---

[23] It is significant that the word *witness* ($\mu\acute{a}\rho\tau\upsilon\varsigma$), which Jesus uses in reference to the disciples (Acts 1:8) and Himself (John 18:37; cf. Rev. 1:5; 3:14) means "martyr," and is so translated several times in the New Testament (Acts 22:20; Rev. 2:13; 17:6). Though the term originally had reference simply to one witnessing to the truth, it came to be used "for those who seal the seriousness of their witness or confession by death." Kittel, op. cit., IV, p. 505. The distinction between *witness* and *martyr* begins to emerge in the second century, though as late as the fifth century the two are still used interchangeably. Augustine, about 416, commenting on the term *witness* in 1 John 1:2, wrote: "Christian lips utter this word daily, and would that this name were also in our hearts, so that we imitated the constancy of the martyrs in their sufferings. The martyrs were God's witnesses." Tract. in Ep., Jo. 1, 2, quoted in Jerome Aixala, *Witnessing and Martyrdom* (Bombay: St. Paul Publications, 1969), p. 92.

we must give ourselves to the purpose for which He died. Love cannot be self-contained any more than it can be stingy. Wherever there is need we must minister in His name according to the gifts and talents God has given.

The demands of discipleship require that we live in a state of spiritual mobilization, bringing our thoughts into the same captivity as the obedience of Christ.[24] Reflecting this commitment is a strict discipline and simple life-style, unencumbered with the things this world seeks, that we might give our maximum energy to God's mission.[25] In the same spirit, we should hold our material resources with an open hand, recognizing that they belong to Christ, and are His to use for the furtherance of the Gospel.

Whoever wishes to go this way will find that it demands daring faith, called fanaticism by sophisticated earthlings but known as joyous freedom by the sons of God. Jesus is looking for such persons to follow Him—disciples who will throw caution to the wind and live like fools for His sake; saintly stalwarts "who laugh at limits, rather do not see them, would not heed them if [they] did"; [26] a peculiar breed indeed, who, like Augustine, entreat the Lord: "Give what you command, and command what you will . . . . O Love that always burns and is never extinguished! O Love that is my God, set me afire!" [27]

---

[24] For a graphic description of the kind of commitment needed in discipleship, I think the most illustrative treatment which I have read is Douglas Hyde's *Dedication and Leadership* (Notre Dame: University of Notre Dame, 1966). This former Communist official tells how Communism trains its leaders for world revolution. Parallels with the pattern of Jesus are striking. Both are driven by a compelling sense of mission, and both demand much the same obedience, except that in Jesus' way it is love infused into the heart by the Holy Spirit that motivates the action. If Christians would take to heart the call of Christ as seriously as the Communists follow their plan of world conquest, then we would soon see the great commission fulfilled.

[25] To me, one of the most challenging aspects of the Lausanne Covenant says: "Those of us who live in affluent circumstances accept our duty to develop a simple life-style in order to contribute more generously to both relief and evangelism" (Section 9).

[26] Amy Carmichael, *God's Missionary* (London: Society for Promoting Christian Knowledge, 1957), p. 17.

[27] Sherwood Eliot Wirt, *Love Song*, the translation of Augustine's Confessions for Modern Man (New York: Harper and Row, 1971), p. 126.

*Hereafter shall the Son of man sit on
the right hand of the power of God.*
Luke 22:69

6

His Heavenly Vision

In His consciousness of mission, with its inevitable cross,
Jesus never entertained the notion of failure. He could see the
glory of the coming Kingdom. His life was filled with triumph
in that joyous anticipation. This is the beautiful note upon
which we will conclude our study.

Eternal Victory

Jesus looked at life from the vantage point of eternity. There
was no uncertainty about the future. The realities of the age to
come dominated His mind every minute. His first coming into
the world to die as the sacrificial Lamb was never isolated
from His second coming to reign as the triumphant King.[1] This
does not mean that He expected the end of the world in His
lifetime, as some have imagined, but merely that He was ever
mindful of His destiny.

This perspective gave eternal meaning to everything that
happened. History was not viewed as a sequence of unrelated
events, but a movement directed toward the goal of its
Creator. He realized that even the power of a perverted man
like Pilate could not be experienced apart from the permissive
will of His Father (John 19:11). By seeing the long-term view
of things, He knew that evil would run its course in this world

___

[1] The fact of the triumphant return of Christ supersedes any interpretation of the events surrounding it, including views of the
tribulation, rapture, and millennium. No purpose would be served in
this study by attempting to argue for one position against another.
What is emphasized here pertains to the basic eschatological outlook
of Jesus, regardless of how it comes to pass.

(Matt. 13:39, 40, 49; cf. 10:22; 24:6, 13, 14); there would be a new age when the chosen of God could truly experience everlasting life (Mark 10:30; cf. Matt. 12:32).

Seeing the joy that was beyond, Jesus accepted without murmur the sufferings of the cross, disregarding its shame (Heb. 12:2). He could wait for His honor among men. Though His appointed way was hard, still the trials of His life could not be compared with the glory which was to be revealed. Others spoke of the ignominy and torture of His death, but never Jesus. To Him this was His glorification, the time when the Father's work was finished, and He could at last return to that glory which was His before the worlds were made (John 12:23, 27, 28; 13:31, 32; 17:1, 5).[2]

The Coming Glory

His Resurrection was the introduction of this new day. How the thought of it must have thrilled His heart! He knew that foolish men would do their worst, venting their anger upon His body at Calvary. Yet as the Scriptures said, His soul would not die (Ps. 49:15; 118:17, 18), nor His flesh see corruption (Ps. 16:10). What appeared to be His total defeat was in reality His greatest victory. Death had no more dominion over Him (Ps. 16:9, 10; Heb. 7:27). For on the third day after His body was sealed in the tomb, He would rise again.

Often He spoke of it with the disciples, the references being most specific when He talked about His impending death (Matt. 16:21; 17:9, 23; 20:19; 26:32; Mark 8:31; 9:9; 10:34; 14:28; Luke 18:33; 24:7, 46). Veiled allusions to the Resurrection appear all through His teaching, like the figure of the

---

[2] Jesus' view of His death gives a fascinating insight to our own experience. For those identified with Christ, death is merely the release of the body previously held in bondage to this world. All the physical consequences of sin are finished, and we are made ready to enjoy eternal life. This does not mean that death erases our bodily existence, but only that our spirit is no longer bound by the limitations of matter. In the Christian's resurrection, his body is changed into a body like that of Christ in His Resurrection (Phil. 3:4; 1 Cor. 15:44, 49; 2 Cor. 5:2; Col. 3:4). However, more than our body is changed in glorification. The term also indicates the state into which we are made partakers of the Spirit of God, even the glory of our Lord.

temple, destroyed by men and yet raised up in three days
(Matt. 26:61; 27:40; Mark 14:58; 15:29; John 2:19). In His
mind, crucifixion and Resurrection were inseparable. "I lay
down my life," He said, "that I might take it again" (John
10:17)—and taking it again, He knew He would bring release
to those who all their days were in bondage to death. He was
the mighty conqueror, who, in death-rending power, would
call back to man, "O child of fear, behold your destiny!" As
"the resurrection and the life," all who believe in Him,
though they die, shall live again (John 11:25, 26)!

His victory over the grave was but the prelude to assuming
His exalted state, when He would ascend back to heaven
(John 6:62; 20:17), and take His place at the right hand of God
(Luke 22:69; 24:51; Mark 16:19; Acts 1:9; 5:31; Eph. 4:8). In
the presence of the Most High, He would reign upon the
throne, His glorified body becoming His people's access to
the holiest (Heb. 10:19, 20).

The heavenly session will be consummated in His triumphant return. Jesus saw Himself coming like lightning flash-
ing across the sky (Luke 17:24; Matt. 24:27) with His holy
angels "in the clouds of heaven with power and great glory"
(Matt. 24:30; cf. 16:27; 25:31; Mark 8:38; 13:26; Luke 9:26;
21:27). He will send forth His angels with a mighty trumpet
blast, and gather the elect from the farthest reaches of the
earth to the uttermost part of heaven (Matt. 24:31; Mark
13:27). Then sitting at the right hand of power (Matt. 19:28;
26:64; Mark 14:62), He will rule in righteousness, putting all
His enemies under His feet.

All these events merge into the coming glory. The time
sequence was not of great importance to Jesus. Nor did He
elaborate upon details. But the joyous assurance of His conquest and exaltation rang through His whole life.

Son of Man

This assurance shines through His constant references to
Himself as the Son of Man.[3] The title relates to the One in

---

[3] Jesus uses this term more than any other when referring to Himself. And with the exception of Acts 7:56, it is found only in His
sayings. Altogether there are eighty-two occurrences of the descrip-

human form foreseen by Daniel who "with the clouds of heaven" came to "the Ancient of days," and "there was given him dominion, and glory, and a kingdom, that all people, nations, and languages should serve him." The prophet adds that "his dominion is an everlasting dominion, which shall not pass away, and his kingdom that which shall not be destroyed" (Dan. 7:13, 14).

In the interpretation of Daniel's vision, the "Son of Man" is identified with "the saints of the most High" who, though greatly oppressed, finally triumph over all the earth, and receive a Kingdom which shall not pass away (Dan. 7:15–28). While much about the passage remains unclear, one cannot mistake its dominant note, which is the ultimate victory of the apocalyptic Son of Man and of those associated with Him.[4] In

---

tion in thirty-six parallel accounts. Outside the parables and beatitudes, it seems well distributed through the Gospels. The fact that Jesus speaks of the Son of Man in the third person can be understood when the term is seen in its common apocalyptic association. Not surprisingly, form critics generally conjecture that the title was ascribed to Him by the later Christian community. Some, like Bultmann, accept the authenticity of the words, but contend that Jesus was referring to someone other than Himself. This notion is untenable, especially in light of such an expression as "I the Son of man" in Matthew 16:13 (cf. Mark 8:27). Jesus leaves no doubt; He is talking about Himself. Much has been written on this subject, one of the most competent general treatments being by the Norwegian scholar, S. Mowinckel, *He That Cometh*, trans. G. W. Anderson (New York: Abingdon, 1954), pp. 346–450. For a listing of many other resources, see the bibliography in George Eldon Ladd, *A Theology of the New Testament*, pp. 145, 146.

[4] In regard to this passage, some view the Son of Man as a symbol representing a people devoted to their heavenly King. Examples are T. W. Manson, *The Teaching of Jesus* (Cambridge: At the University Press, 1963 © 1931), p. 227, cf. 211–236; and George Duncan, *Jesus, Son of Man* (New York: Macmillan, 1949), p. 148. However, as F. F. Bruce observes, an association with the saints need not rule out His individual personage, *The New Testament Development of Old Testament Themes* (Grand Rapids: Wm. B. Eerdmans, 1968), p. 26. As to the suffering implied in the vindication of the people of God, again there are diverse opinions among scholars. See F. F. Bruce, Ibid., p. 29; C. F. D. Moule, *The Phenomenon of the New Testament* (Naperville, Ill.: Alec R. Allenson, Inc., 1967), pp. 32–42, 82–99; and Morna D. Hooker, *The Son of Man in Mark* (London: S.P.C.K., 1976), pp. 11–32.

spite of the suffering involved, this exalted supernatural person is destined to reign in the consummation of time.

The noncanonical Jewish literature of the time cast the Son of Man in the same light. It saw Him as a preexistent heavenly Being who would descend to the earth, destroy the ungodly, deliver the righteous, and rule a never-ending kingdom of holiness in fellowship with His subjects. Though the expectation had some of the same ingredients as the popular Messiah-warrior who would overthrow paganism, this Messianic figure also has the qualities of the universal divine Saviour and the Servant of God.[5]

Within this context, yet bringing into it new meaning, Jesus alluded to His earthly ministry. He pictured Himself coming from heaven as the Son of Man (John 3:13) and in that exalted state going about His mission of sowing the good seed and seeking the lost (Matt. 13:32; Luke 19:10). What difference did it make that He lived in lowly circumstances? He was still the Son of man (Matt. 11:19; Luke 7:34). When the disciples were rebuked for plucking corn unlawfully, He responded with the same refrain, "For the Son of man is Lord even of the sabbath day" (Matt. 12:8; Mark 2:28; Luke 6:5). In His own right "the Son of man" had authority to forgive sins (Matt. 9:6; Mark 2:10; Luke 5:24); execute judgment (John 5:27); and give everlasting life (John 6:27). When He spoke of His rejection, betrayal, and crucifixion, He was aware that "the Son of

---

[5] This is brought out particularly in the pseudepigraphal books of Enoch 38:2; 39:6; 40:5; 46:2–6; 48:1–7; 53:6; 62:1–16; 69:26–29; and IV Ezra 13:3, 26, 32, 37, 38, 52; 14:9. R. H. Charles, ed., *The Apocrypha and Pseudepigrapha of the Old Testament*, II (Oxford: At the Clarendon Press, 1913). A comparison of these references with Messianic promises in Isaiah may be found in Joachim Jeremias, *New Testament Theology*, p. 272. We do not know to what extent Jesus relied upon the extrabiblical sources, but they would have been familiar to many Jews, and thus provided a context for His use of the term. This is discussed by T. W. Manson, in "The Son of Man in Daniel, Enoch and the Gospels," *Bulletin of the John Ryland's Library*, XXXII, 2 (March, 1950), pp. 171–193; and Matthew Black, "The Son of Man in the Old Biblical Literature," *Expository Times*, LX, 1 (October, 1948), pp. 11–15; and by the same author, "The Eschatology of the Similitudes of Enoch," *Journal of Theological Studies*, New Series, III, 1 (April, 1952), pp. 1–10.

man" would suffer these things (Matt. 17:12, 22; 20:28; 26:24, 45; Mark 8:31; 9:12, 31; 10:45; 14:21, 41; Luke 9:22, 44; 22:22; John 3:14; 6:53; 8:28; 12:23). Of course, He would die, but the grave could not hold "the Son of man" (Matt. 17:9; 20:19; Mark 9:9; 10:34; Luke 18:31).

Every time He used this name, it was more than a prophecy of His coming rule; it indicated that in His mind that rule was already a reality. He never thought of Himself in any other way. Even when no one else seemed to understand, He was no less the Son of Man—the mighty conqueror over evil, destined to rule the universe with invincible holy love.

The Kingdom of God

Jesus' announcement that the Kingdom of God was at hand accented this victorious consciousness (Matt. 4:17, 23; Mark 1:15; Luke 4:43). In proclaiming this truth, He focused on a theme which runs through the whole of Scripture—God reigns over His people.[6] Of course, God is inherently King over all nations (2 Kings 19:15; Isa. 6:5; Jer. 46:18; Ps. 29:10; 47:2; 96:10; 99:1-4; 145:11), but in a special sense He was King of Israel (Exod. 15:17, 18; Deut. 33:5; Isa. 43:15), working in their history to show His glory. However, the Kingdom had never been fully realized in their experience. The anticipated universal reign of God awaited the Messianic age when their King would come to rule over all the nations.

Jesus saw this promise in fulfillment. That which had been given in covenant, embodied in the Law, typified in Israel's government, and envisioned by the prophets, was personified in His life and work. In His mind the Kingdom had come and

---

[6] In recent years this subject has received considerable attention from biblical scholars, resulting in a plethora of literature. A comprehensive and readable study of its historical development, particularly in the Old Testament, is John Bright, *The Kingdom of God* (New York: Abingdon-Cokesbury, 1953). An evangelical writer in this area who deserves special mention is George Eldon Ladd, particularly his *Crucial Questions About the Kingdom of God* (Grand Rapids: Wm B. Eerdmans, 1968, © 1952); and *Jesus and the Kingdom* (New York: Harper and Row, 1964). The latter book includes a good bibliography of the pertinent writing in this field.

was coming. What Oscar Cullman calls the "already" and "not yet" both existed in Him.[7]

It is present in the salvation sense of spiritual reality whenever the King is loved and served (Luke 17:20, 21; cf. 16:16; Matt. 18:3; John 3:5). Thus, like a treasure of incalculable value, the Kingdom can be possessed now. But one will have to give up everything to obtain it (Matt. 13:44–46). Only those who are desperately in earnest, who storm its gates with violence, will get in (Matt. 11:12; cf. Luke 16:17).[8] Still, the

---

[7] Oscar Cullman, *Salvation in History* (London: SCM Press, 1965), pp. 166–236. The present and future aspect of the Kingdom exist in tension, and are not mutually exclusive. However, many scholars have emphasized one to the exclusion of the other, or at least, made the other secondary. Johannes Weiss and Albert Schweitzer, for example, insist that Jesus meant the Kingdom was wholly futuristic, a view which has come to be known as "consistent eschatology." Some also hold that Jesus expected the fulfillment in His lifetime, and when it did not happen, He was left in despair. Modifications of this basic idea will be seen in Rudolf Bultmann, R. H. Fuller, M. Werner, among others. Reacting to this school, some believe that the Kingdom has no eschatological reference, but is present in people who are doing God's will. Following this logic, they see Jesus as the supreme example of obedience, and His mission as essentially that of bringing others into the same life. Variations of this view will be found in T. W. Manson, F. C. Grant, J. W. Bowman, and the "realized eschatology" of C. H. Dodd. But in taking only one of these emphases the biblical evidence supporting the other side has to be explained away, an approach always unsatisfactory. The best way to deal with the problem is to treat all the evidence objectively, maintaining the truth of both ideas. Most recent interpreters follow this course, such as J. A. Baird, John Bright, C. E. B. Cranfield, F. V. Filson, and Donald Guthrie, to mention a few.

[8] This intriguing passage can be variously interpreted. The verb βιάζεται may be seen passively, meaning that the Kingdom suffers violence from its enemies, either human or demonic. Some even see an allusion to misguided revolutionists, like the Zealots. More likely, however, the word should be interpreted in the middle voice, conveying the idea of the Kingdom exercising its mighty power by the way it came violently into the world. In this context, it might point to the ministry begun by John the Baptist, and completed by Christ, whereby the old order of things was assaulted, and multitudes were brought to hear the Gospel. More generally applied, men of zeal grasp the Kingdom, like those that storm a city, carrying off its spoils. While a definitive word cannot be given, no one can doubt that the Kingdom demands daring boldness, and those that are its champions

Kingdom can never be achieved by human ingenuity; it comes as a gift from God (Matt. 21:43; Luke 12:32).

The Kingdom is mysterious in the manner it comes quietly into the world, almost without being recognized. Jesus compares it to seed growing in different soils, depicting the different ways the Word of God may be received (Matt. 13:3–23; Mark 4:3–20; Luke 8:5–15). Again it is likened to a mustard seed, beginning very insignificantly, but growing to become a tree (Matt. 13:31, 32; Mark 4:30–32); or like leaven unseen in the loaf, it gradually permeates the whole (Matt. 13:33). The parable of the tares shows how the true subjects of the Kingdom live alongside the children of this world. Society is not disrupted until the final harvest, when the tares will be cast out (Matt. 13:24–30, 36–43; cf. Mark 4:26–29). That all grow up together is illustrated also in the parable of the net (Matt. 13:47–50). Not until the net is drawn can the good be separated from the bad, and only the Lord will make that differentiation.

Victory Over All

Christ's authority over the demonic world displays the power of His reign. Satan is helpless before Him. The devil still seeks to stop His ministry (e.g., Mark 8:33; Luke 22:3, 31), but Jesus confronts him as a defeated foe—his power is broken, his honor spoiled (Matt. 12:29; Luke 11:21, 22). Following the return of the seventy from their mission of proclaiming the Kingdom and casting out demons, Jesus mentioned having seen Satan fallen like lightning from heaven (Luke 10:18), an allusion to the way the powers of evil would be overthrown.[9]

---

go forth to do mighty exploits for God. Certainly the indifferent and slothful find no peace therein.

[9] Whether Jesus was speaking figuratively or describing an actual vision, the reference points up the spiritual struggle against which His Kingdom is viewed. There is a conflict between the forces of good and evil, light and darkness. As to when Jesus saw the fall of Satan, it could allude to eternity past when Satan was defeated in an attempt to usurp the place of Christ in heaven (cf. Jude 1:6; 2 Pet. 2:4). Some think that it refers to a time during Christ's ministry on earth, perhaps the temptation in the wilderness. Others look at it in a

Though the war is still waging, the decisive battle has been won, and it is only a matter of time before Satan's rule will be completely destroyed.

The victory, already realized by faith, will be visible when the Kingdom comes to fruition in the day of the Lord.[10] Then all the trials of the righteous will be over. Sickness and sorrow will end. Men shall come from the east and west to celebrate the heavenly banquet (Matt. 8:11). The redeemed will be like the angels in immortality (Mark 12:18–27), knowing at last the fulness of His Resurrection (Luke 20:34–36).

His Church

The persons who enter the Kingdom and live under its government form a fellowship of "called-out ones," the Church.[11] Such fellowship is seen in the company of disciples gathered around Jesus, who as the "little flock" (Luke 12:32), carried on

---

futuristic sense in the exclusion of Satan from heaven (Rev. 12:9–11), which Jesus already knew as a fact. In history, however, it would appear that the cross was where the actual deathblow to Satan was dealt (John 12:31; 16:11; cf. Heb. 2:14). Since the past and future were always present in His mind, the time factor really does not matter. What stands out in Luke 10:18 is the relationship between Satan's overthrow and the disciples' ministry. For a treatment of this whole idea, see Oscar Cullman, *Christ and Time,* trans. Floyd V. Filson (Philadelphia: Westminster Press, 1964), pp., 84, 198; and Joachim Jeremias, *New Testament Theology,* p. 95.

[10] "Day of the Lord" has both historical and eschatological significance. In history it is a time of judgment when God acts (Amos 2:5; 3:9–11; 4:12; 5:18–20; Isa. 13:4–6, 17; Zeph. 1:7). Yet it is also a day in the future when God will judge (Amos 7:4; 8:8, 9; 9:5; Isa. 13:11), and a day of salvation for the house of David, when the blessing of Israel will be realized (Amos 9:11–15; Zeph. 3:9–20). The prophets blended the two aspects together, for it is the same God who acts in both. The question of when an event happens is not of primary concern, but rather that God's will be done. The Olivet discourse shows Jesus speaking about the future this way when He uses parabolic pictures and symbolical language to describe future events which transcend our experience. For a discussion of the "Messiah's Day," see Alexander Reese, *The Approaching Advent of Christ* (Grand Rapids: Grand Rapids International Publications, 1975), pp. 167–183.

[11] The question of whether or not the Kingdom is separate from the Church is academic. Those with a dynamic view generally make a distinction between the two, as does Ladd: "The Kingdom is the rule

the mission of the true Israel (Mark 12:1–9; Matt. 8:11, 12; 21:43).[12] Believers become the custodians of the Kingdom, taking the place of those who rejected the King. They are His actual representatives in this world (Matt. 10:9–14), so much so that they are to be treated as one would treat Jesus Himself (Matt. 10:40; Mark 9:37).

As the recipient of the life and mission of Christ, the Church displays to this world the character of the world to come. Though perfect attainment awaits the day when all evil is banished, still the order of heaven establishes the ethic of God's people now.[13] Love for the Son is the rule of conduct.

---

of God; the church is a society of men." *Jesus and the Kingdom,* p. 258. The same idea is held by John Bright, op. cit., p. 236. Some even say that Jesus had no idea of establishing a church, but that it was the Kingdom of God He planned. For example, A. Loisy, *The Gospel and the Church,* trans. Christophere Horne (New York: Charles Scribner's Sons, 1909), p. 166. Dispensationalists like J. F. Walvord, J. B. Pentecost, and A. J. McClain, contend that the Jews rejected the earthly Davidic Kingdom of heaven, which then caused Jesus to form the Church and introduce the idea of the Kingdom of God to all. In this view, the Church has no direct lineage with Israel. However, most scholars follow Augustine and believe that the Kingdom in its spiritual aspects is identical with the Church. See Geerhandus Vos, *The Teaching of Jesus Concerning the Kingdom and the Church* (Grand Rapids: Wm. B. Eerdmans, 1951), pp. 77–90; and James Orr, *The Christian View of God and the World* (Grand Rapids: Wm. B. Eerdmans, 1963 © 1867), p. 358.

[12] The continuity between the disciples of Jesus and the Israel of God is underscored by their designation to sit on twelve thrones "judging the twelve tribes of Israel" (Matt. 19:28; Luke 22:30). The number twelve also reflects the congregation of God. Ladd believes, too, that the "little flock" is an allusion to the Old Testament concept of Israel as the sheep of God's pasture (Isa. 40:11). *New Testament Theology,* p. 108. For a comprehensive treatment of the Church in relation to the covenant people of Israel, see Richard R. DeRidder, *Discipling the Nations* (Grand Rapids: Baker, 1975). The book also includes a good bibliography.

[13] Albert Schweitzer advanced the idea that the Kingdom ethic was supraethical, that is in the future when distinctions of right and wrong are unnecessary. In the brief period before that time, he believed, an "interim ethic" was in effect, which was essentially repentance and moral reform. *The Mystery of the Kingdom of God* (New York: The Macmillan Co., 1950 © 1901), pp. 53–72. I find no biblical support for this view. Conduct should reflect the character of God's rule, whether now or in the future.

Man's self-centered ego has no place. In this morality, human behavior manifests the character of Christ by joyfully accepting His Law. Since self-seeking is gone, there is no clamor for recognition. The Church has no ambition but to see her Lord exalted, who alone is worthy of praise.

Jesus could see the coming evangelization of the world through this ministering body of disciples. He knew that His servants would continue His work, giving as they had received (Matt. 10:7, 8; Luke 9:2; 10:9), until the Gospel of the Kingdom was heard by "all nations" (Matt. 24:14; cf. Mark 13:10).[14] The faithful, by virtue of their knowledge of revelation, would open the way for all men to be saved, so that through their message they would bind on earth what was bound in heaven (Matt. 16:19; 18:18; cf. John 20:23).[15] This witness, typified in Peter's affirmation of faith, was the rock upon which Christ was building the Church, and "the gates of hell shall not prevail against it" (Matt. 16:18).[16] The powers of

---

[14] For an able treatment of this expectation of the whole earth's coming under the dominion of Christ, a basic concept in the theology of missions, see Johannes Blauw, *The Missionary Nature of the Church* (New York: McGraw-Hill Book Company, 1962); and Joachim Jeremias, *Jesus' Promise to the Nations* (Naperville: Alec R. Allenson, Inc., 1958).

[15] In rabbinical tradition a teacher, on the strength of his knowledge of the Law, would declare something "bound" or "loosed," meaning that it was forbidden or permitted. Hence, it could be said that one who adheres strictly to the truth taught by Christ can make decisions which will be ratified in heaven. This principle extends even to the matter of forgiving or retaining sin by declaring a thing lawful or unlawful. It is a strong injunction, not only for church discipline, but for clear proclamation of the Word of God. For acceptance of the saving truth of the Gospel looses one from sin's guilt and penalty, while rejection leaves the sinner in bondage. The authority to bind or loose is not inherent in man, however lofty his station, but it is dependent upon the revelation of truth perceived in Christ. See A. T. Robertson, *Word Pictures in the New Testament* (New York: Richard R. Smith, 1930), I, p. 135; and John Peter Lange, *Commentary on the Holy Scriptures* (Grand Rapids: Zondervan, n.d.), Matthew, pp. 298, 299, 329.

[16] Jesus picks up on the Hebrew idea of building a people, again a familiar theme through the Old Testament (Jer. 1:10; 24:6; 31:4; 33:7; Ps. 118:22; Amos 9:11; Ruth 4:11). As to the rock itself, there is wide discrepancy as to what it means. Some see the rock as Christ Himself;

death would be broken by their testimony. Nothing could permanently defeat them. Whether the reference was to a final conquest in the end time, or the conflict with evil that will continue up to the end, the victory is assured.

Joy of Heaven

No wonder Christ's life was filled with gladness. God was raising up sons to praise Him forever. They would inherit the Kingdom prepared from the foundation of the world (Matt. 25:34; cf. Rom. 8:17; Gal. 3:29; Titus 3:7; Heb. 1:14; 6:17; Col. 1:12; Acts 20:32; 26:18). Their names were written in heaven (Luke 10:20). Visions of this holy people who would behold His glory strengthened Him as He contemplated the future (John 17:5, 24). To think of the love which they would share! And the communion feast which they would celebrate at the table of the Lord (Matt. 8:11).

Heaven was real to Him. The singing of the angelic chorus around the Throne of Grace echoed through His mind.[17] The sound of the silver trumpets ringing through the streets of gold was vibrant in His soul. Sometimes when He felt that the people around Him did not realize what He was doing, He would receive consolation in the knowledge that the courts of heaven understood. He knew that there was "joy in the presence of the angels of God over one sinner" who repented (Luke 15:10). When His disciples did not appreciate the attention given to little children, Jesus reminded them that in

---

others see it as the orthodox doctrine that He is the Son of God; while still others relate it to Peter, either as an individual or the representative spokesman of the Church. The fact remains, however, that it was not until after Peter expressed what he believed that Jesus mentioned building His Church upon the rock. That is why, however interpreted, evangelism cannot be separated from this foundation. Only as men hear of Christ, and believe on Him, can the Church be raised up. Moreover, without such witness, there would be no Church in the next generation.

[17] It is well to note that Jesus found the existence of angels, like demons, very real. Several times mention is made of their ministry to Him, particularly in times of exhaustion (Matt. 4:11; Mark 1:13; Luke 22:43). That He was conscious of their readiness to help was apparent at His arrest, when He said that, had He asked, "twelve legions of angels" would have come to His assistance (Matt. 26:53).

heaven their angels beheld the face of His Father (Matt. 18:10). Peter, James, and John did not want their Lord to talk about being killed, but when He was transfigured on the Mount, as if for a moment in heaven, He found it easy to discuss His death with Moses and Elijah, "who appeared in glory" (Luke 9:31). In this heavenly atmosphere He was at home.

Jesus had no illusions about this world. He was fully aware that He was a misfit here, just as those who would take His words to heart. But this world was not His home—His mansions were in another country (John 14:2), a place of resplendent love and unspeakable joy, where rust could never tarnish nor evil men defile.

The Blessed Hope

Jesus taught the disciples to view their present ministries with this same anticipation. He wanted them to have His long look, and to live in the radiance of the coming glory. The Kingdom was something which they could "see" now by faith in Christ (John 3:3, 5). And on the day of its consummation they would "see heaven open, and the angels of God ascending and descending upon the Son of man" (John 1:51). Thereafter they would sit with Him on the throne of His glory (Matt. 19:28).

One might think that the disciples would have jumped up and down in excitement at this prospect. But such was not the case. Having only a faint understanding of the cross, the resurrection life seemed far removed from them. In fact, even after the crucifixion and burial of Jesus, it was hard for them to believe until they saw His glorified body (Matt. 28:9, 17; Mark 16:9; Luke 24:15, 26, 50; John 20:19, 26; 21:1; cf. 1 Cor. 15:5, 6, 7, 8; Acts 9:5). Until then their understanding of the Kingdom still reflected the popular earthbound expectations of the people (Acts 1:6).

But as the wonder of Easter morning flooded in upon them, and especially as they were filled with the Holy Spirit, the glory of their risen, ascended, and reigning Lord permeated their witness. They lived and died in the joyous certainty of the Kingdom, giving themselves without reserve to its proclamation. Nothing else seemed so relevant. However far along they were in bringing the Gospel to the world, they lived with their eyes fixed on heaven, "looking for that blessed hope, and the glorious appearing of the great God and our Saviour Jesus Christ" (Titus 2:13).

Living in Readiness

Nevertheless, we can understand why the disciples asked their Lord, "When shall these things be? and what sign will there be when these things shall come to pass?" (Luke 21:7; cf. Matt. 24:3; Mark 13:4). It was natural for them, as it is for us, to want a well-defined time schedule, especially in view of the momentous events which were to transpire.

How Jesus answered the disciples in the Olivet discourse reflects again upon His sense of values (Matt. 24:1–25, 36, 46; Mark 13:1–37; Luke 21:5–36). He tells them that it was not necessary for them to know the precise time of His coming. An exact knowledge, in fact, might have detracted from the primary need to live in constant anticipation and readiness. Hence, He reminded them that no one knows the day or hour, not the angels of heaven, not even Jesus in the human side of His nature. That information is reserved for deity alone (Matt. 24:35, 42, 44; 25:13; Mark 13:32; cf. Acts 1:7).

Jesus did, however, point to some general signs of the end time, particularly in reference to the calamities leading up to the fall of Jerusalem and the abominations of desolation spoken of by Daniel (Matt. 24:15; Mark 13:14; cf. Dan. 9:27; 11:31; 12:11). Still, it is not clear whether or not the allusions to wars, famines, and pestilences, spoken of in connection with the end, refer to the end of the age or to the events surrounding the destruction of Jerusalem in A.D. 70.[18] Reaching the whole world with the Gospel is also prophesied as

---

[18] This is not surprising when it is considered that the disciples' questions which led to the Olivet discourse concerned both the time of the Temple's destruction and Christ's return. Some like to associate the first thirteen verses of Matthew 24 and Mark 13 with the first-century period, and the later portions to the end of the age. Others, observing that Jesus did not indicate which part of His answer related to which aspect of the questions, refer the whole discourse to both periods. In this view, the judgments which fell upon Jerusalem in A.D. 70 are a foreshadowing of the situation prior to the Lord's Second Coming.

something to take place before the end will come (Matt. 24:14;
cf. Mark 13:10), though again what this means is not clear.[19]
Then there is that reference to the budding of the fig tree,
which points to the renewing of the nation of Israel (Matt.
24:32–34; Mark 13:28–30; Luke 21:29–32). Jesus said that the
generation which sees this happen will not pass away "till all
these things be fulfilled." But what comprises this generation,[20] and how much of the prophetic events must they witness?

Since Jesus did not give a specific interpretation Himself, a
variety of deductions are possible, none of which can be asserted with finality. Yet, for this very reason, no one should
assume that the return of the Lord necessarily must be de-
layed. We should live as if He were coming today. The call is
to watchfulness and diligence. It is enough to know that the
Lord is coming. Until then, we must be about His work.
"Blessed is that servant whom his master when he comes will
find so doing" (Matt. 24:46 RSV).[21]

[19] For example, do radio broadcasts around the world meet this
requirement? If such is the case, then the prophecy is being fulfilled.
Others insist, however, that the Gospel was preached to all nations of
the world in the first century (Acts 8:4; Col. 1:5, 6). On the other
hand, how do we account for those tribal groups which, so far as we
know, have not yet heard the good news in their own tongues? This
leads many to believe that the promised return of Christ awaits the
translation of the message into all languages, and its proclamation to
every tribe.

[20] Those who see the restoration of Israel today as the fulfillment of
this prophecy like to believe that within this generation, or a span of
thirty to forty years, Christ will return. However, "generation" does
not have to be interpreted in relation to time, for it can also refer to a
race of people. Thus, the passage may be saying that the Jewish race
will continue until all the prophecies concerning Christ's return are
fulfilled. A very interesting discussion of this idea within the larger
context of the other aspects of Jesus' prophecies is in Franz Mussner,
Christ and the End of the World, translated by Maria von Eroes
(Notre Dame: University of Notre Dame Press, 1965).

[21] Most people it seems will not be ready when the Lord comes.
The certainty of the King's return holds no challenge for them. They
are like the people of Noah's day, going about their usual activity—
eating, drinking, marrying—but oblivious to their imminent doom
(Matt. 24:37–39). Jesus' parables of the porter, the faithful and evil
servants, the ten virgins, and the talents also warn of this prevailing
attitude at His coming (Matt. 24:42—25:30; Mark 13:35–37; Luke
12:36–40).

Reward of the Faithful

There can be no doubt that whenever Christ does return every person shall give account according to His works (Matt. 16:27; cf. Rom. 2:6; 2 Cor. 5:10; 1 Peter 1:17; Rev. 20:12; 22:12). "Before him shall be gathered all nations" (Matt. 25:32; cf. John 5:22; cf. Acts 17:31; Rom. 2:16; 2 Tim. 4:1). Every idle word will be weighed (Matt. 12:36). To whom much is given; much shall be required (Luke 12:48).

For the unbelieving, of course, this is a fearful day; but to the King's servants who are ready, there is no apprehension. The coming judgment will be merely the vindication of those heavenly values which believers already cherish. We will then be known even as we are known; our labor for the Master, unseen now by men, will receive at last its just recompense (Matt. 6:1, 4, 18; Luke 14:14). The servant who is faithful to his Lord's trust will gain his reward (Matt. 25:14–30; Luke 19:11–27), inheriting the Kingdom prepared from the foundation of the world (Matt. 25:31–40).

This does not mean that one deserves heaven's favor, for at best we know ourselves to be unprofitable servants (Luke 17:10). Everything that is received of God is of grace (Matt. 20:1–16). Christian work is never motivated by a sense of earning merit. Indeed, one who seeks personal gain will lose it (Luke 17:33). When Jesus spoke of those on His right hand receiving the Kingdom, the righteous seemed taken by surprise, "when saw we . . . ," so removed is the thought of reward from their service (Matt. 25:37–39). Nevertheless, God will judge our works, and in His own "good pleasure" (Luke 12:32), He will give the appropriate reward (Matt. 5:12). That which is done in love for His glory will never be lost.

We can labor with this confidence. Neither the opinions of uncaring critics nor the bias of admiring friends should be of great concern. We have only One to judge us, and to Him alone must we bow. What we do now can only be assessed by heaven's values. Jesus has taught us that our treasures are not in this world, but in the world to come.

O Happy Day

So let us set our affection on things above (Col. 3:1, 2). Our true citizenship is there. We belong to the King. Whether we live or die, we are in His keeping. Already we sit with Him in heavenly places (Eph. 2:6), and each passing hour brings us closer to that day when faith shall turn to sight (1 Cor. 13:12). While it does not yet appear what we shall be, "We know that, when he shall appear, we shall be like him; for we shall see him as he is" (1 John 3:2; cf. Isa. 33:17; Rev. 22:4).

In this brief period before His return, our occupation is in the fields white unto harvest where the Spirit is gathering the Church. What does it matter that the work is hard? The end will justify every sacrifice. Tears shed on earth will be pearls in heaven. They that go forth with weeping shall doubtless come again, rejoicing and bringing their sheaves with them (Ps. 126:6).

It comes as no surprise that the world remains indifferent, or even hostile, to our witness. In fact, as the end approaches, conditions may get a lot worse than they are now. Before it is over, those who are faithful will be openly harassed, many even killed. But God's program will not suffer defeat. He will win the last battle. Rather than be distracted by the struggle, let us fix our attention upon the victory.

The King is coming! Looking toward that glorious event, we live like a young bride waiting for her wedding day. Every moment hastens the happy union soon to be consummated. Excitement fills our common toil. We walk on tiptoe, laughing and singing and praising God. To think that soon we shall be presented to our Beloved in eternal wedlock! Just the thought makes the heart almost skip a beat in wonder.

Someday the trumpet will sound and Jesus Himself shall descend from heaven with a shout, in trailing clouds of glory (1 Thess. 4:16). Before Him every knee shall bow, in the realms above and on the earth below, and every tongue shall confess that He is Lord (Phil. 2:10, 11). All creation shall worship before Him, and His judgments shall be manifest (Rev. 15:4). The kingdoms of this world will become the Kingdoms of our God. He shall reign, King of kings and Lord of lords, from hallelujah to hallelujah, forever and forever (Rev. 11:15; 17:14; 19:1, 3, 6).

"Even so, come, Lord Jesus" (Rev. 22:20).

Epilogue

Evangelism centers in a Personality— Jesus Christ. He is the message and the medium. The Gospel mandate and its reproduction is wedded to His life.

Obviously then, any person who learns of Him will become evangelistic, just as the discipleship out of which it grows will be developed. Some of what this involves has been briefly sketched in these pages. But if it is to mean anything more than words, we must seek to apply these principles to our own lives.

Enabling of the Spirit

Basic to everything else, of course, is the inner reality of the living Saviour. No one can live a life he does not have. It is not a matter of trying to imitate Christ, but of simply believing Him to live out His life in us.

The experience of this fact makes us witnesses of divine grace. Our lives become an epistle of the Lord, "written not with ink, but with the Spirit of the living God; not in tables of stone, but in fleshy tables of the heart" (2 Cor. 3:3). One so transformed creates a mystery in the world, which causes other persons to turn aside and behold the wonder. This visible demonstration not only validates the Gospel, it also establishes the basis for an ongoing life of discipling men by bidding them to follow us as we follow the Lord (1 Cor. 11:1; Phil. 3:17; 4:9; 2 Thess. 3:7; 2 Tim. 1:13).

Naturally the countless deficiencies in our fallen nature, involuntary though they may be, bring reproach upon our witness. Yet the consciousness of our limitations urges us to surrender what we know of ourselves to the Spirit's control. He is our Comforter, our Guide, our Strength, always making real Christ's presence in our midst. By confessing anything which hinders His possession of us and by emptying out every thought of our self-sufficiency, we can by faith receive the promise of the Father. Every child of God can live in the

fulness of Pentecost.[1] Not that we have no further need of
refining, or that we can contain all that He wants to give, but
that all we are can be in His keeping.

Here each one of us must face the issue. Are we truly living
in conformity to the Son of God? Though there is continual
maturing in His likeness, can we say now, as we understand
our own hearts, that we love Him supremely? And thereby do
we love ourselves in Him, even as we love our neighbor? In
such a person the Holy Spirit is sure to manifest the life and
work of Jesus.

The Work of Prayer

This accents the imperative of prayer—"the inbreathing of
the life of God in the soul of man." [2] There can be no spiritual

---

[1] The unique historical setting of the Spirit's outpouring at Pentecost makes difficult any experiential definition of its equivalent today. Some, for example, would see this event as an initial conversion.
Others look upon it as a spiritual effusion subsequent to regeneration. That the experience may not be continuous adds to the
difficulty. Perhaps it could be agreed that everyone receives the
Spirit when saved, though the fulness of the Spirit may not be
realized until later, nor the conditions maintained. However interpreted, what matters is that the Spirit have undisputed reign in the
heart. To see how this principle pertains, one might profitably consult some of the popular readings on this subject by representative
leaders, such as Samuel Logan Brengle, *When the Holy Ghost Is
Come* (New York: Salvation Army Printing and Publishing House,
1911); Samuel Chadwick, *The Way to Pentecost* (New York: Fleming
H. Revell, 1932); Billy Graham, "How to Be Filled with the Holy
Spirit," *Revival in Our Time* (Wheaton: Van Kampers, 1950, pp.
105–121); Andrew Murray, *The Full Blessing of Pentecost* (London:
Oliphants Ltd., 1954); J. Edwin Orr, *Full Surrender* (London: Mar-
shall, Morgan & Scott, 1951); and R. A. Torrey, *The Baptism of the
Holy Spirit* (New York: Fleming H. Revell, 1895). Among others who
have variously written about this quality of life within their own
theological context, to all of whom I am debtor, are: John Wesley,
Blaise Pascal, Jonathan Edwards, Brother Lawrence, Francais Fene-
lon, C. T. Studd, Charles G. Finney, V. R. Edman, Hudson Taylor,
Emile Cailliet, Oswald Chambers, E. Stanley Jones, H. C. Morrison,
Phoebe Palmer, Ian Thomas, A. B. Simpson, Sidlow Baxter, Francis
Asbury, William Booth, F. B. Meyer, Vance Havner, Hannah Whitall
Smith, Myron Augsburger, Bill Bright, Horatius Bonar, Thomas Up-
ham, L. E. Maxwell, A. W. Tozer, Paul Rees, and John Church. The
student of Christ could well afford to spend some time with these
sensitive hearts.
[2] Octavius Winslow, op. cit., p. 178.

communion without it. The movement of the Spirit in and through us will be no greater than the degree to which we pray.

We must learn to wait in the presence of the Holy One, to meditate upon His attributes, to bask in the sunlight of His love, to worship Him in the beauty of His holiness. In this atmosphere, we can bare our souls, knowing that God understands us as we are and is able to supply all our needs. Here, we also fulfill our highest priesthood, when we intercede on behalf of others for whom Christ died.

The ideal is to maintain a constant attitude of prayer, so that in every task we are conscious of divine fellowship. For this to mean much in practice, however, we need to establish some set periods for devotion. Most crucial is the scheduled quiet time when we shut out the distractions of the world and meet with the Father in secret. This becomes the sweetest part of every day.[3] Other personal disciplines, like fasting,[4] also

---

[3] Information on the practice of personal devotion is plentiful and generally accessible. Those who have made notable contributions to this field during the past century include: Thomas A. Carruth, Samuel Chadwick, Dietrich Bonhoeffer, Andrew Murray, Charles L. Allan, William E. Sangster, Armin Gesswein, J. W. Acker, Herbert Lockyer, J. Neville Ward, G. Campbell Morgan, Peter Green, R. A. Torrey, Vonette Bright, Louise Eggleston, George S. Stewart, Oswald Chambers, Harry E. Jessop, John Baillie, John R. Rice, Edgar N. Jackson, F. J. Huegel, Frank Laubach, Samuel Zwemer, Ralph Martin, John McGee, Reginald F. Goff, Harold Lindsell, among many others. A few practical and representative books are Charles Wheston, *Pray: A Study of Distinctively Christian Praying* (Grand Rapids: Wm. B. Eerdmans, 1953); S. D. Gordon, *Quiet Talks on Prayer* (New York: Grosset and Dunlap, 1941); and Albert C. Wieand, *The Gospel of Prayer* (Grand Rapids: Wm. B. Eerdmans, 1953). Of the older works, two that have been especially helpful to me are Matthew Henry, *The Secret of Communion with God*, written in 1712, now reprinted, edited by Elizabeth Elliot (Old Tappan, N.J.: Fleming H. Revell, 1963); and William Law's classic, *A Serious Call to a Devout and Holy Life*, first published in 1729, and still in print (New York: E. P. Dutton, 1972). For a current bibliography in this field, contact The Department of Prayer and Spiritual Life, Asbury Theological Seminary, Wilmore, Kentucky 40390.

[4] Fasting, like any religious discipline, can be easily perverted. Wrongly observed, it leads to undue asceticism, even hypocrisy. Doubtless this has caused many in the Church to avoid its practice. However, where its purpose is kept in view—to sensitize spiritual perception through self-denial—abstinence can prove a great blessing. Those who would like an objective presentation of the subject, especially in its practical application, will appreciate the writings of

might be observed to further emphasize the spiritual dimension of life. Each person will have to find his own style. Though the pulse of prayer may be weak in the beginning, one can be sure that it will grow in strength and meaning as he matures in Christ.

In addition to these private exercises, we need time to pray with members of the Body of Christ. Some of these associations are quite small, as in the family and with little groups of friends.[5] Other meetings involve the whole congregation of believers. No Christian should ever neglect the assembling of the saints, especially when the purpose is to pray.

Unfortunately, under the pressure of so many demands, we may let vital communion slip to the periphery of our schedule. If we find this happening, surely we have our priorities out of order. It is not really a question of time, but of values. We always make time for those things which we consider most important. One thing is sure: Only as we pray in the Name of Christ will the radiance of the upper room fill our daily toil.

Under Authority

To keep devotion from becoming subjective, communion with the Spirit must be grounded in the written Word of God. This is foundational to everything that we do, for the Word is the objective basis of our knowledge of Christ, and thus, His ministry.

Every disciple of Christ should resolve to be "a man of one

Arthur Wallis, Derek Prince, Thomas Carruth, and Paul C. Bragg. As an introduction, I suggest James Lee Beall, *The Adventure of Fasting* (Old Tappan, N.J.: Fleming H. Revell, 1974), and David R. Smith, *Fasting, A Neglected Discipline* (Fort Washington: Christian Literature Crusade, 1944). The latter book includes a good bibliography, mostly of older works, where supplementary information may be found.

[5] There is no scarcity of material relative to group praying. In addition to many of those writing in the area of personal communion, the following authors offer practical counsel in the dynamics of group praying: John L. Casteel, Glenn Clark, Douglas Steere, Samuel Emerick, Harold W. Freer, Steve Harper, Francis B. Hall, Elton Trueblood, Ron Dunn, Charles W. Shedd, Herbert A. Thelen, Reul Howe, Harrison S. Elliott, Walden Howard, Elizabeth O'Conner, and Lyman Coleman. To get a feel of this practice, one might read for insight Helen Shoemaker, *Power Through Prayer Groups* (Westwood, N.J.: Fleming H. Revell, 1958); and Rosalind Rinker, *Prayer: Conversing With God* (Grand Rapids: Zondervan, 1959).

book." [6] It is not that other books are ignored, but that our preeminent concern is to learn the precepts of the one Book inspired by God. Our minds should be so enmeshed in Scripture that we unconsciously think in the same thought patterns until "the very essence of the Bible flows through" our being.[7]

Such saturation does not come without effort. As a minimum, we need to read consistently, following some plan that assures coverage of the total biblical message. We should also have regular periods for intensive study, when we probe the deeper meaning of the text, utilizing the skills of induction and exposition.[8] Selected passages should also be memorized, permitting instant recall and constant reflection.[9]

[6] John Wesley, *The Letters of the Reverend John Wesley*, A.M., IV (London: The Epworth Press, 1931), p. 299.

[7] C. H. Spurgeon, quoted in Richard Ellsworth Day, *The Shadow of the Broad Brim* (Philadelphia: Judson, 1934), p. 131.

[8] Any Christian can learn to rightly divide the Scriptures by following basic principles of exegesis. If one needs help in this area, he should consult with someone whose competence has been demonstrated. The student might also peruse some of the literature in this field, including A. T. Pierson, *Knowing the Scriptures* (New York: Gospel Publishing House, 1910); Wilbur Smith, *Profitable Bible Study* (Boston: W. A. Wilde Co., 1939); Howard T. Kuest, *These Words Upon Thy Heart* (Richmond: John Knox Press, 1947); Lloyd M. Perry, Walden Howard, *How to Study Your Bible* (Old Tappan, N.J.: Fleming H. Revell, 1957); Oletta Wald, *The Joy of Discovery* (Minneapolis: Bible Banner Press, 1956); and, most of all, Robert A. Traina, *Methodical Bible Study* (New York: Gaines & Harris, 1952). Other teachers who have written notable works are: James M. Gray, Charles Augustus Briggs, Oswalt Allis Thompson, Joseph Gettys, R. A. Torrey, G. Campbell Morgan, Albert Edwin Avery, W. H. Griffith-Thomas, Josiah Blake Tidwell, Bernard Ramm, Samuel Ridout, Merrill Tenney, Milton Terry, Howard F. Vos, George Turner, H. Clay Trumbull, J. W. Weddell, R. B. Gindlestone, Henrietta C. Mears, John P. Oakes, to name only a few. A man deserving special note is Wilbert W. White, whose vision for training Christian workers is told by Charles R. Eberhart in *The Bible in the Making of Ministers* (New York: The Association Press, 1949). An annotated bibliography for Bible-study methods appears in Perry and Howard, op. cit., pp. 201–218.

[9] Practical help in Scripture memorization can be secured from the Navigators, Memory Ministries, Gideons, Bill Gothard Seminars, Christian Outreach, and The Bible Memory Association, among others. Some books describing this discipline are by William Evans, *How to Memorize* (Chicago: Bible Institute Colportage Association, 1910); Oscar Lowry, *Scripture Memorizing for Successful Soul-*

Mastering the Scriptures, of course, requires being mastered by them. No amount of knowledge can compensate for submission to the truth. Without this commitment, we fall into the same delusion as the religious gentry of Jesus' day, making zeal for the letter of the Law an occasion for self-vindication and vain glory. Learning God's Word implies a teachable spirit. This means approaching the Bible with a receptive mind and a readiness to obey the Spirit. Spiritual illumination is given to those who seek the Lord with their whole hearts. Such are the true disciples of Christ. They have direction and authority in their lives, and following their Lord, they do not cease to show others the way to God.

Knowing the Gospel

In the Scripture we learn of the Saviour, but we also learn who man is and what he can become by the power of God. This knowledge not only brings us to repentance and faith in Christ, but it also thrusts us out to tell the way of salvation to those who still languish in the quagmire of sin.

The nonchalant way that so many of us go about evangelism may make one question if we actually comprehend the depths to which man has fallen. Or is it the other way around? Perhaps we have no real concept of the infinite heights to which man can ascend through God's grace. Whatever the problem, fuzzy thinking at this point is deadening. Not only must we understand the essential truth of the Gospel, but we must be able to articulate it clearly to the world.[10]

Winning (Grand Rapids: Zondervan, 1932); and Norman Lewis, *Bible Themes Memory Plan* (Lincoln: Back to the Bible, 1964). A few simple rules for both Bible study and memorization are summarized in my book, *Life in the Living Word* (Old Tappan, N.J.: Fleming H. Revell, 1975), pp. 87–99.

[10] If help is needed at this point, there is in the voluminous apologetic literature something to suit any taste. Among some of the more popular books are those of C. S. Lewis, *Mere Christianity* (New York: Macmillan, 1952); John Stott, *Basic Christianity* (Grand Rapids: Wm. B. Eerdmans, 1958); and Josh McDowell, *Evidence That Demands a Verdict* (San Bernardino: Campus Crusade for Christ, 1972). More in the theological vein are works by A. Skevington Wood, *Evangelism: Its Theology and Practice* (Grand Rapids: Zondervan, 1966); Ralph W. Quere, *Evangelical Witness* (Minneapolis: Augsburg, 1975); Francis A. Schaeffer, *Escape From Reason* (Chicago: InterVarsity, 1968); and D. James Kennedy, *Truths That Transform* (Old Tappan, N.J.: Fleming H. Revell, 1974). In addition to these contemporary

Believing the revelation commits us to proclaiming it. If we do not do this where we have opportunity, we are accomplices in the lost's tragic ignorance—their blood is on our hands (Acts 20:26; Ezek. 33:8, 9). From the standpoint of moral obligation, how can we be indifferent knowing that immortal souls are perishing without the Saviour? What does it matter that some may not care? The question is, Do we? Evangelistic concern is not based upon appreciation, but upon truth. If mankind is not totally lost, or if recovery of man's fallen nature can come through some means other than the blood of Christ, then of course, there is no need to take evangelism seriously. But if the claims of the Gospel are true, and Jesus offers the only way into the Kingdom of God, then making this fact known is at the core of our very existence.[11]

Purposeful Love

This necessity to evangelize gives direction to the unfolding plan of our life. How it finds expression will depend upon

writings the student might read some of the older classics, such as Joseph Alleine, *An Alarm to the Unconverted* (New York: American Tract Society, 1850); Richard Baxter, *A Call to the Unconverted* (New York: American Tract Society, 1830); and the work of John Angell James, *The Anxious Inquirer after Salvation* (Philadelphia: Presbyterian Board of Publication, n.d.). Though tedious for modern readers, these timeworn writings provoke serious thought.

[11] One who would like to learn more about vocal witnessing is advised to go out with someone who is effective. There are, of course, any number of training books and manuals which may be profitably consulted. If I were to select a few representative treatments for special mention, among them would be Bill Bright, *How to Introduce Others to Christ* (San Bernardino: Campus Crusade for Christ, 1968); Paul Little, *How to Give Away Your Faith* (Downers Grove: InterVarsity, 1966); James Kennedy, *Evangelism Explosion* (Wheaton: Tyndale, 1970); Howard G. Hendricks, *Say It With Love* (Wheaton: Victor, 1972); Nate Krupp, *You Can Be a Soul Winner—Here's How* (Chicago: Lay Evangelism, Inc., 1962); and Dr. Desumi Toyotome, *The Manual of the Nameless Movement* (Manila: Christian Literature Crusade, 1968). In connection with this effort at communication, it would be well also to read *What's Gone Wrong With the Harvest?* by James F. Engel and H. Wilbert Norton (Grand Rapids: Zondervan, 1975). A general listing of materials, including many in the field of personal soul-winning, may be found in Roy Fish, *Study Guide to the Master Plan of Evangelism* (Old Tappan, N.J.: Fleming H. Revell, 1972), pp. 61–65; and the revised edition of George E. Sweazey, *Effective Evangelism* (New York: Harper & Row, 1976), pp. 277–281.

personal gifts and circumstances, but whatever our particular situation, all of us have a place in the reconciling mission of Christ. Everything we do is seen against the background of God's purpose to redeem the world.

We cannot fulfill this purpose and remain out of touch. To minister in His stead we must get next to people, sharing their lowly estate, bearing their sorrows, and carrying their griefs. In the process, there will be conflict with those who would oppress the weak, and though we have no enthusiasm for revolution, we cannot avoid working for reform. The kind of holiness that we experience in Christ is fearless in contending for righteousness.

Yet we do not cast our lot with the society of this world, though we feel the weight of its burdens. Our loyalty is to Christ, whose Kingdom we proclaim, even as we lead that little group around us into the life pattern of the great commission.[12] Pouring our life into a few learning hearts, teaching

---

[12] Published material pertaining especially to skills of discipling is not nearly as plentiful as writing on soul winning, though the field is developing. Deserving of attention is Walter A. Henrichsen, *Disciples Are Made—Not Born* (Wheaton: Victor, 1973); Gary A. Kuhne, *The Dynamics of Personal Follow-up* (Grand Rapids: Zondervan, 1976); Winkie Pratney, *Youth Aflame* (Auckland: Communication Foundation, 1967); *A Guidebook to Discipleship* by Doug Hartman and Doug Southerland (Irvine, Calif.: Harvest House, 1976); and Carl Wilson, *With Christ in the School of Disciple Building* (Grand Rapids: Zondervan, 1976). Also considerable help can be found in related areas, like leadership development, as in *The Art of Management for Christian Leaders* by Edward R. Dayton and Ted W. Engstrom (Waco: Word, 1976). Another is in counseling, of which Dr. Gary Collins, *How to Be a People Helper* (Santa Ana: Vision House, 1976) is a good example. Some who have written about evangelistic training, such as Jim Kennedy, LeRoy Eims, Howard Hendricks, Ralph Neighbors, and Jack Voelkel, have made significant contributions. Of those who have described it from the standpoint of equipping laymen for ministry, Carlos Ortez, *Disciple* (Carol Stream: Creation House, 1975) is most refreshing. Others who have written in this field include Stuart Briscoe, George H. Harvey, Bob Smith, Jim Wallis, Stanley R. Hoyt, Charles R. Stewart, J. Dwight Pentecost, Larry Richards, Mendall Taylor, Waylon Moore, Malcolm Smith, and Lyell Rader. There is, too, the literature on Church renewal, especially that related to the small-group movement, which offers insight. On the personal level, one will find a variety of resources that encourage discipline and growth, of which *My Spiritual Notebook* by Billy Hanks, Jr. (Waco: Word, 1974), used in his Christian Discipleship Seminar, is one of the best.

them in turn to make disciples, while not spectacular in its immediate results, will bring untold compensation in generations to come.

The love of Christ keeps prodding us on. In His bonds there is no discharge from duty. Nor can there be any escape from hardship and pain. Love makes one vulnerable, for it does not seek its own, but seeks the good of its beloved. Herein is its joy. If we find ourselves grumbling in adversity, then we had better look more closely within our hearts to see how deeply we feel the love wherewith we are loved.

Finally God does not want our service, but our devotion—the free offering of ourselves to Him in gratitude for His unspeakable gift. Embracing the cross brings us to revel in pouring out life at the feet of Jesus. A faith without this commitment is a self-contradiction, and may well appear to others as a fraud. The proof that we believe what Jesus says is that we are willing to venture everything for His cause. His glory, and His glory alone, is the obsession and delight of our soul.

The Coming Glory

Such dedication is utter foolishness to the world, of course. But to those who are crucified with Christ, it is the wisdom and the power of God. What unbelief cannot see is that on the other side of Calvary is the open tomb, and the fulness of everlasting life. When once we glimpse those things which are eternal, the sufferings and trials of this present age are as nothing.

Though it may appear now that the events around us display a spirit of rebellion, we can be sure that God is working through every circumstance to accomplish His will. The Kingdom is coming, and through the eyes of Christ, we can live in the spirit of that coming glory now.

We go into the world with the assurance that our Lord's purchased possession will be gathered from "every kindred, and tongue, and people, and nation" (Rev. 5:9; cf. 7:9). In the schedule of heaven it is already announced—the great commission is fulfilled; the celebration has begun. Evangelism simply directs our energy toward that inevitable goal to which history is moving, when the completed body, the blood-washed Bride of Christ, will be presented unto the Father in witness to the glory of His grace.

Until then we live as pilgrims in an alien land. There is no place here for our spirits to dwell. We seek a city which has foundations in the heavens. In this anticipation, our longing eyes turn toward the eastern skies, looking to that time when our majestic Saviour, crowned with glory and honor, returns to rule over all. In that eternal day we shall live in the light of His countenance, and with that host which no man can number, in perfect solidarity of love, serve Him in perpetual praise!

This is more than a hope. It is the unshakable affirmation that Jesus Christ has taken unto Himself His own great power, and His dominion is forever. With this vision ever before us, let us press the claims of the Kingdom. The Lord God Almighty reigns, and with Him, we, too, are more than conquerors.

> Jesus, the very thought of Thee
> With sweetness fills my breast;
> But sweeter far Thy face to see
> And in Thy presence rest.
>
> Nor voice can sing, nor heart can frame,
> Nor can the mem'ry find
> A sweeter sound than Thy blest name,
> O Savior of mankind!
>
> O hope of ev'ry contrite heart,
> O joy of all the meek,
> To those who fall how kind Thou art!
> How good to those who seek!
>
> But what to those who find? Ah, this
> Nor tongue nor pen can show—
> The love of Jesus, what it is
> None but His loved ones know.
>
> Jesus, our only joy be Thou,
> As Thou our prize wilt be;
> Jesus, be Thou our glory now
> And thru eternity.[13]

---

[13] Latin, twelfth-century hymn, trans. by Edward Caswall.